McGRAW-HILL READING

# Language Support

**Grade 2**     Lessons/Practice/Blackline Masters

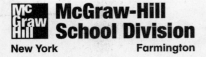
**McGraw-Hill
School Division**

New York     Farmington

# Table of Contents

## Grade 2

Introduction .................................................................. v-xviii

## Unit 1

**Ann's First Day** ...................................................................1-9
  Graphic Organizer: Blackline Master 1 .................................................5
  Build Skills: Blackline Masters 2-5 ..................................................6-9

**Henry and Mudge** ...............................................................10-18
  Graphic Organizer: Blackline Master 6.................................................14
  Build Skills: Blackline Masters 7-10 ..............................................15-18

**Luka's Quilt** ...................................................................19-27
  Graphic Organizer: Blackline Master 11 ..............................................23
  Build Skills: Blackline Masters 12-15 .............................................24-27

**Roundup at Rio Ranch** ..........................................................28-36
  Graphic Organizer: Blackline Master 16 ..............................................32
  Build Skills: Blackline Masters 17-20 .............................................33-36

**Welcome to a New Museum** .......................................................37-45
  Graphic Organizer: Blackline Master 21 ..............................................41
  Build Skills: Blackline Masters 22-25 .............................................42-45

## Unit 2

**Lemonade for Sale** .............................................................46-54
  Graphic Organizer: Blackline Master 26 ..............................................50
  Build Skills: Blackline Masters 27-30 .............................................51-54

**A Letter to Amy** ...............................................................55-63
  Graphic Organizer: Blackline Master 31 ..............................................59
  Build Skills: Blackline Masters 32-35 .............................................60-63

**Splash!** .......................................................................64-72
  Graphic Organizer: Blackline Master 36 ..............................................68
  Build Skills: Blackline Masters 37-40 .............................................69-72

**Jamaica Tag-Along** .............................................................73-81
  Graphic Organizer: Blackline Master 41 ..............................................77
  Build Skills: Blackline Masters 42-45 .............................................78-81

**Sharks** ........................................................................82-90
  Graphic Organizer: Blackline Master 46 ..............................................86
  Build Skills: Blackline Masters 47-50 .............................................87-90

# Unit 3

**Arthur Writes a Story** . . . . . . . . . . . . . . . . . . . . . . . . . . . . . . . . . . . . . . . . . . . . . **91-99**
  Graphic Organizer: Blackline Master 51 . . . . . . . . . . . . . . . . . . . . . . . . . . . . . . . .95
  Build Skills: Blackline Masters 52-55 . . . . . . . . . . . . . . . . . . . . . . . . . . . . . .96-99

**Best Wishes, Ed** . . . . . . . . . . . . . . . . . . . . . . . . . . . . . . . . . . . . . . . . . . . . . . . **100-108**
  Graphic Organizer: Blackline Master 56 . . . . . . . . . . . . . . . . . . . . . . . . . . . . . . .104
  Build Skills: Blackline Masters 57-60 . . . . . . . . . . . . . . . . . . . . . . . . . . . . .105-108

**The Pony Express** . . . . . . . . . . . . . . . . . . . . . . . . . . . . . . . . . . . . . . . . . . . . . . **109-117**
  Graphic Organizer: Blackline Master 61 . . . . . . . . . . . . . . . . . . . . . . . . . . . . . . .113
  Build Skills: Blackline Masters 62-65 . . . . . . . . . . . . . . . . . . . . . . . . . . . . .114-117

**Nine-in-One, Grr! Grr!** . . . . . . . . . . . . . . . . . . . . . . . . . . . . . . . . . . . . . . . . . . **118-126**
  Graphic Organizer: Blackline Master 66 . . . . . . . . . . . . . . . . . . . . . . . . . . . . . . .122
  Build Skills: Blackline Masters 67-70 . . . . . . . . . . . . . . . . . . . . . . . . . . . . .123-126

**Change for the Quarter** . . . . . . . . . . . . . . . . . . . . . . . . . . . . . . . . . . . . . . . . . **127-135**
  Graphic Organizer: Blackline Master 71 . . . . . . . . . . . . . . . . . . . . . . . . . . . . . . .131
  Build Skills: Blackline Masters 72-75 . . . . . . . . . . . . . . . . . . . . . . . . . . . . .132-135

# Book 2 Unit 1

**Charlie Anderson** . . . . . . . . . . . . . . . . . . . . . . . . . . . . . . . . . . . . . . . . . . . . . . . **136-144**
  Graphic Organizer: Blackline Master 76 . . . . . . . . . . . . . . . . . . . . . . . . . . . . . . .140
  Build Skills: Blackline Masters 77-80 . . . . . . . . . . . . . . . . . . . . . . . . . . . . .141-144

**Fernando's Gift** . . . . . . . . . . . . . . . . . . . . . . . . . . . . . . . . . . . . . . . . . . . . . . . . **145-153**
  Graphic Organizer: Blackline Master 81 . . . . . . . . . . . . . . . . . . . . . . . . . . . . . . .149
  Build Skills: Blackline Masters 82-85 . . . . . . . . . . . . . . . . . . . . . . . . . . . . .150-153

**Best Vacation Ever** . . . . . . . . . . . . . . . . . . . . . . . . . . . . . . . . . . . . . . . . . . . . **154-162**
  Graphic Organizer: Blackline Master 86 . . . . . . . . . . . . . . . . . . . . . . . . . . . . . . .158
  Build Skills: Blackline Masters 87-90 . . . . . . . . . . . . . . . . . . . . . . . . . . . . .159-162

**Zipping, Zapping, Zooming Bats** . . . . . . . . . . . . . . . . . . . . . . . . . . . . . . . . . **163-171**
  Graphic Organizer: Blackline Master 91 . . . . . . . . . . . . . . . . . . . . . . . . . . . . . . .167
  Build Skills: Blackline Masters 92-95 . . . . . . . . . . . . . . . . . . . . . . . . . . . . .168-171

**Going Batty for Bats** . . . . . . . . . . . . . . . . . . . . . . . . . . . . . . . . . . . . . . . . . . . **172-180**
  Graphic Organizer: Blackline Master 96 . . . . . . . . . . . . . . . . . . . . . . . . . . . . . . .176
  Build Skills: Blackline Masters 97-100 . . . . . . . . . . . . . . . . . . . . . . . . . . . .177-180

## Book 2 Unit 2

**Bremen Town Musicians** ...................................................**181-189**
   Graphic Organizer: Blackline Master 101 ...........................................185
   Build Skills: Blackline Masters 102-105...................................186-189

**Our Soccer League**........................................................**190-198**
   Graphic Organizer: Blackline Master 106 ...........................................194
   Build Skills: Blackline Masters 107-110...................................195-198

**The Wednesday Surprise**................................................**199-207**
   Graphic Organizer: Blackline Master 111 ...........................................203
   Build Skills: Blackline Masters 112-115...................................204-207

**Fossils Tell of Long Ago**................................................**208-216**
   Graphic Organizer: Blackline Master 116 ...........................................212
   Build Skills: Blackline Masters 117-120...................................213-216

**Are You a Fossil Fan?**...................................................**217-225**
   Graphic Organizer: Blackline Master 121 ...........................................221
   Build Skills: Blackline Masters 122-125...................................222-225

## Book 2 Unit 3

**Officer Buckle and Gloria**...............................................**226-234**
   Graphic Organizer: Blackline Master 126 ...........................................230
   Build Skills: Blackline Masters 127-130...................................231-234

**Tomas and the Library Lady** ...........................................**235-243**
   Graphic Organizer: Blackline Master 131 ...........................................239
   Build Skills: Blackline Masters 132-135...................................240-243

**Princess Pooh** ..........................................................**244-252**
   Graphic Organizer: Blackline Master 136 ...........................................248
   Build Skills: Blackline Masters 137-140...................................249-252

**Swimmy** ................................................................**253-261**
   Graphic Organizer: Blackline Master 141 ...........................................257
   Build Skills: Blackline Masters 142-145...................................258-261

**The World's Plants Are In Danger** .....................................**262-270**
   Graphic Organizer: Blackline Master 146 ...........................................266
   Build Skills: Blackline Masters 147-150...................................267-270

# INTRODUCTION

As a dynamic social process, learning calls for students and teachers to be partners. This Language Support Manual, which accompanies MCGRAW-HILL READING, was developed to help you achieve that partnership.

Throughout this Language Support Manual you will find strategies and activities designed to help ESL students become participants in classroom learning communities with their English-speaking peers. Based on current and proven methods for teaching ESL students, these strategies and activities reflect important ideas about the learner's role and about language and communication, which are at the heart of MCGRAW-HILL READING.

For ease of reference, this introduction is divided into two parts: the first part, **Teaching the ESL Student**, is designed to orient you to the unique needs of the ESL learner; and the second part, **Teaching the Reading Selection**, mirrors the corresponding lesson in the Teacher's Edition and offers suggestions on how to present the reading skills and concepts for classes with native speakers and second language students.

**Students and teachers are partners in learning.**

**Sheltered Instruction**

## Teaching the ESL Student

This section of the introduction will help you adapt your skills to meet the needs of the ESL student. Differences between teaching native English speakers and ESL students are linguistic, social, and cultural. It is not enough for ESL students to know the appropriate language to use in a given context, although this is certainly critical. In addition, you, as teacher, must ensure that ESL students are active and equal participants in the classroom. Students must be made to feel that their contributions are valuable even though they may only approximate native English speaker accuracy. They must also feel that their culture and prior experience have a respected place in the classroom.

In the following chart, we provide you with the characteristics of language learners in each of the four stages of second language acquisition. You will find it useful in identifying language behavior and building a profile of your ESL students. In the remainder of this section, we will outline procedures and activities for accommodating ESL students, strategies for meeting their unique needs, group interaction patterns that foster effective learning, the classroom environment, assessment tools, and social factors and their relevance to learning.

# Stages of Second-Language Acquisition

Like their English-speaking classmates, ESL students will be at different levels of language and literacy proficiency in their native language. They will also be in various stages of English language acquisition. This Language Support Manual lists teaching prompts at four different levels which follow the chart below and summarizes the four stages of second language acquisition. As your ESL students move through the four stages, this chart may be helpful in making informal assessments of their language ability and in determining which prompts you should use.

**nonverbal prompt for active participation**

## Preproduction
- Teachers ask students to communicate with gestures, actions, yes/no answers, and names.
- Lessons focus on listening comprehension.
- Lessons build receptive vocabulary.

(Reading and writing are incorporated.)

**one- or two- word response prompt**

## Early Production
- Teachers ask students to respond to *either/or* questions.
- Students respond with one or two word phrases.
- Lessons expand receptive vocabulary.
- Activities encourage students to produce vocabulary they already understand.

(Reading and writing are incorporated.)

**prompt for short answers to higher-level thinking skills**

## Speech Emergence
- Students respond in longer phrases or sentences.
- Teachers model correct language forms.
- Lessons continue to develop receptive vocabulary.

(Reading and writing are incorporated.)

**prompt for detailed answers to higher-level thinking skills**

## Intermediate Fluency
- Students engage in conversation and produce connected narrative.
- Teachers model correct language forms.
- Reading and writing are incorporated.

# Procedures and Activities

**Scaffolding Process**

The teacher's role in the scaffolding process is to provide necessary and meaningful support toward each learning objective. The scaffolding process requires the student to take ownership for learning and the teacher to provide appropriate direction and support in teaching. It requires a form of collaboration between teachers and students in which both work together to ensure that students internalize rules and strategies for meaning-making. The following components of sheltered language instruction are methods which support the needs of second language learners and provide for optimal language arts learning.

- Reciprocal Teaching
- Cooperative Grouping
- Cross-age Tutoring

**Reciprocal Teaching**

Reciprocal teaching is one way to help ESL students successfully complete academic tasks. The process of reciprocal teaching involves structuring an interaction, assessing the student's comprehension from the response, and then restructuring the interaction to clarify or correct the student's response. As with other kinds of interactions in the classroom, *reciprocal teaching should be modeled and practiced as a whole class first, then it should be practiced in pairs.* The following are just some of the benefits which occur when this approach is implemented in the classroom.

- Teachers can show students not only what to learn but how to learn.
- Group interaction lends itself to varied learning styles.
- Students accept new responsibilities through a cooperative approach.
- Students' self-esteem is enhanced through shared responsibilities.
- Collaborative learning yields greater motivation, particularly for students at risk.

**Cooperative Grouping**

Through cooperative grouping, which is also very collaborative, students gradually assume responsibility for their learning. This approach is most effective when there is individual accountability. *Cooperative learning best provides the non-native speaker with opportunities similar to social experiences within which the native speakers have acquired the language.*

**Cross-age Tutoring**

The cross-age tutoring format provides yet another opportunity for students to study and learn together. *ESL students benefit from cross-age tutoring as they are engaged in focused conversation that will support their second language development.* Cross-age or peer tutoring has also been found to promote positive reading attitudes and habits.

Reciprocal teaching, cooperative grouping, and cross-age tutoring are approaches within the pedagogical framework of sheltered English instruction. The benefit of these varied grouping formats is that group members become interested in each other's opinions, feelings and interests. ESL students begin to feel more comfortable expressing themselves on the topic or in the presentation.

# Successful Group Interaction

*How do I insure that ESL students participate?*

**nonverbal prompt for active participation**

Being sensitive to the cultural backgrounds of ESL students is a critical function of the teacher. In many cultures, the teacher has absolute authority in the classroom and students play a relatively passive role. Students from such cultures may not participate as vigorously as their classmates.

**Elicit experiences that relate to students' native cultures.**

By creating a safe environment both in the classroom, and within the group structure, students will begin to participate more freely. You may facilitate this by eliciting experiences and including activities that relate to students' native cultures. For example, if you are discussing the weather, have students talk about the weather in their countries and ask them to bring in pictures that show the range of weather in their country. Ask such questions as: *Draw a picture of a rainy and cloudy day in your country.* This Language Support Manual offers many opportunities to incorporate individual cultural backgrounds. Every lesson includes activity suggestions and teaching prompts which introduce skills and strategies through a compare/contrast matrix in the **Evaluate Prior Knowledge** and **Develop Oral Language** sections.

*How should I group my native English students and ESL students for maximum learning and cooperation?*

**ESL students benefit from social interactions with native speakers.**

Social interaction plays an important role in language development. In group work, ESL students benefit from interactions with native speakers by having more chances to try out the language they are learning. But effective group work depends on careful organization, thoughtful selection of groups, and the active involvement of the teacher.

Additionally, the following chart details various strategies that can enhance both reading comprehension as well as the oral language proficiency of second language learners.

# A Pedagogical Overview of Strategic Sheltered Instruction

| SCAFFOLD | APPROPRIATE TASKS | BENEFIT TO THE READER |
|---|---|---|
| **Modeling** | Teacher models task and provides examples. Individual/Group oral reading, repetitions. Direct experience through practice. | Clarifies concepts Provides understanding of objective |
| **Connecting Content** | Questions in: Think-Pair-Share Three-Step Interview Quick-Writes Anticipatory Charts Brainstorming | Addresses students' prior knowledge Provides a personal connection between learner and theme of the class |
| **Creating a Context** | Visualizations Focus questions and: Use of manipulatives Self-involvement Instructor provides an experiential environment. Students demonstrate knowledge for authentic audiences. | Enhances context and concept familiarity |
| **Bridging Concepts** | Compare/Contrast Matrix used as advanced organizer Story Graph used to skim through a text | Students gain heightened insight of the varied uses of the language. Students develop connections between concepts. |
| **Perceptual Understanding** | Reciprocal Teaching Self-monitoring Self-assessment Students discuss and model reading strategies | Self-autonomy is fostered Enhances students' knowledge of strategies through a conscious focus on the processes |
| **Extension** | Drama Journal writing Story Boards Collaborative posters with text Eye-witness accounts Post cards/letters | Students extend their understandings and personal relevance as they apply information to novel formats. |

## Modeling

*How do I adapt my teaching methods to accommodate the ESL learner?*

**Illustrate the Concept**

In addition to traditional board work, ESL students need a significant amount more support and practice than native English speakers. Therefore it is essential that you give those students the necessary practice and it is vital that this support comes in the form of experiential and oral activities, before written work or reading. For example, writing the words *big* and *small* on the board and then asking students to name objects in either category, is not an adequate presentation for ESL learners. A more successful technique would be to illustrate the concepts through the use of physical objects in the room. For example, taking words that have already been associated with their objects, the teacher points to the larger of the two and says *This is big.* The students then repeat the phrase after the teacher's model. Next, the teacher points to the smaller object and says This is small. The students respond as in the previous example. The teacher can then point to two other objects (or pictures), one big and one small. Given the teacher's cue, the students point to and classify the two objects as either big or small.

By assisting the learner in producing utterances beyond his or her capacity, you are providing 'scaffolding'—that is, the necessary support and guidance needed for the learner's growth. Through this collaboration of teacher and student, the student should progress towards greater autonomy and ownership of his or her language, thereby fostering greater self-esteem and independence.

## Total Physical Response

*What activities should I use to supplement teaching?*

ESL students need to cover concepts using a variety of sensory input. Total Physical Response (TPR) is a well-established and successful technique that links language to a physical response. The classic game of "Simon Says" is a vivid example. The teacher (or a student) can call out a series of commands (i.e., "Simon says, touch your toes,") and students respond with the appropriate physical gesture—in this case, by touching their toes. The advantage of this technique is it links language to the "here and now," giving learners, especially at the early stages, a concrete forum for language practice.

Because of linguistic, social, and cultural differences, ESL students will probably not cover concepts as quickly as native English speaking students. The teacher must be patient with these students and give them extra activities with varied sensory input. As with all learners, varying the pace and type of sensory input is essential—both for accommodating the various learning style preferences and maintaining interest in the lesson.

# Suggested TPR Commands

| | | |
|---|---|---|
| Stand up | Giggle | Turn your head to the *right* |
| Sit down | Make a face | Drum your fingers |
| Touch the *floor* | Flex your muscles | Wet your lips |
| Raise your *arm* | Wave to *me* | Blow a kiss |
| Put down your *arm* | Shrug your shoulders | Cough |
| Pat your *cheek* | Tickle your *side* | Sneeze |
| Wipe your *face* | Clap your hands | Shout *your name* ("help") |
| Scratch your *knee* | Point to the *ceiling* | Spell *your name* |
| Massage your *neck* | Cry | Laugh |
| Stretch | Yawn | Sing |
| Whisper *(a word)* | Hum | Hop on *one foot* |
| Step *forward* | Lean *backwards* | Make a fist |
| Shake your *hand* | (Name), walk to the door | (Name), turn on the *lights.* |

Source: Richard-Amato, P. (1996) Making it happen: *Interaction in the second-language classroom,* 2nd ed. White Plains, N.Y.: Addison-Wesley Publishing Group/Longman.

# Connecting Content

**Don't assume that ESL students don't know the answer.**

*How do I know my ESL students understand me?*

When you question your students and get no answer don't automatically conclude that students don't know the answer. Adapt your questioning strategies to help ESL students understand what you say. Rephrase the question. Replace difficult vocabulary with words students know. Add context by using pictures, objects, graphic organizers to support meaning. Use gestures and facial expressions to cue feelings and moods. Draw analogies to past experiences.

# Creating A Context

**Use of Manipulatives**

The Language Support Manual includes several blackline masters which coincide with the skills and strategies being taught within a reading selection. The blackline masters provide manipulatives to help students explore and practice skills. Use of manipulatives helps to enhance context while building concept familiarity.

*How do I set up the classroom as a strategic learning environment?*

**The Classroom Environment**

The environment of the classroom can have a great impact on students' ability to learn. The following are some ways to make the classroom environment more comfortable so that ESL students can get as much as possible out of their classroom experiences.

**Special areas in the room provide chances for students to apply their English skills.**

Create areas in the room designed to give ESL students opportunities to use the target language. For instance, if you are teaching the names of fruits, set up a "fruit market" and have students ask the "shopkeeper" for the fruits they want to buy. They can talk about how the fruits look and taste, how to prepare them, and how much they cost.

Set up a learner library with favorite books the students have chosen. Provide a "discussion" area where ESL students may sit with native language speakers to discuss their favorite books or to read to each other. Seating arrangements should always provide for flexible grouping.

# Bridging Concepts

*How do I activate 'prior knowledge' for students from a different culture?*

With native English speaking students, the teacher has common ground on which to activate the students' prior knowledge. Although American culture is very diverse, there are certain associations and symbols that are familiar to all those who live here. However, for the ESL student the teacher faces a difficult challenge—being able to activate the students' prior knowledge often without knowledge of the students' cultures. With ESL students, as with all students, the teacher should be sure to allow students to make connections for themselves. Often the teacher has a pre-determined idea of the connection and by imposing that notion on the student, he or she does not serve the students' needs to the fullest. It is important for ESL students to develop autonomy and self-esteem.

**Allow ESL students to make connections for themselves.**

# Assessment

*How do I assess ESL learners?*

When assessing ESL students' learning, you need to adapt your expectations of what constitutes an appropriate response. Assessment that relies heavily on a written test or questionnaire, on written answers or an essay, or on answering oral questions verbally, may present problems for ESL students. Some alternative strategies include the following:

**Use alternative ways to assess ESL students' learning.**

- Allow students to draw, show, or point to an object, a procedure, or an illustration, rather than write or talk about it.

**Invite students to draw, show, or point to objects.**

- Use your own observations and interactions with the students as a basis for assessment.

**Your observations may serve as a form of assessment.**

- Ask students to perform an activity that will show the application of a concept. For instance, say: *Show me how a tired person acts.*

**Students may perform activities to demonstrate their understanding.**

# Teaching the Reading Selection to Students Needing Language Support

Each Language Support lesson in this Language Support Teacher's Guide mirrors the corresponding lesson in the Teacher's Edition of McGraw-Hill Reading. It either builds directly on that lesson, offering suggestions on how to adapt materials for students needing additional language support, or it offers alternative teaching and activities. The blackline masters following each lesson provide tools for students to use with alternative activities that develop skills and strategies taught in the lesson.

In this overview, the Language Support lesson described is from the grade one unit theme, Stories to Tell. The selection, *Sam's Song,* is the story of a young owl who learns to sing with her family. Variations on the lesson in Grades K, 3-6 are noted where appropriate.

# Focus on Reading

**Help develop children's awareness of sounds.**

## Develop Phonological Awareness (Grades K-2)

This part of the Language Support lesson is designed to help children develop their ability to hear the sounds in spoken language. These skills can be improved through systematic, explicit instruction involving auditory practice. Each selection in grades K-2 begins with a lesson designed to focus the children's attention on a particular phonological skill. In the grade one selection, for example, children are asked to listen for digraphs, *ch, wh,* and *nk.* As you read aloud the poem, "Lunch Munch," children are asked to clap their hands each time they hear a word that rhyme with *bunch.* The activity is repeated with the word *think.*

Children who may be having difficulty hearing these sounds are guided through an activity in which they make up a series of tongue twisters containing the digraphs. For example: *The child chomps on a chip.* Students listen for and identify the words in which they hear /ch/.

In these practical, learner-centered lessons from the Language Support Teacher's Guide, children are often asked to respond physically to the sounds they hear. For example, in this grade one lesson, they are asked to whistle, chomp, or blink when they hear words with *wh, ch,* or *nk.*

The Language Support Teacher's Manual identifies these activities as **TPR** (Total Physical Response).

One of the most successful approaches to teaching English to language support children is Total Physical Response. At the heart of this approach is the belief that children should be active participants—as both fellow learners and experts—in learning communities where language and content are developed together.

## TPR:

- is most appropriate for children just beginning to speak English. It recognizes that children will spend a period of time—the silent period—listening to English before they are able to speak it. Particularly focused TPR activities help ESL children learn vocabulary and concepts.

- recognizes that ESL children can understand physical prompts and can indicate their understanding through action before speech. TPR involves giving commands in which you model a physical action and to which learners respond with an action, one or two words, or short responses.

- allows children to involve their bodies and their brains in the TPR activity; they respond with the total body. The commands should be fun and should make the second language understandable.

As you work with children needing additional language support , you may find many other ways to use TPR prompts. As children continue to develop their phonological awareness, they will be asked to identify rhyming words, listen for separate syllables in a word, separate the first sound in a word from the rest of the word, and blend sounds together to make words. Recent research findings have strongly concluded that children with good phonological awareness skills are more likely to learn to read well. These lessons will help you work with children from diverse cultural and linguistic backgrounds as well as engage ESL children in productive activities to achieve literacy.

## Develop Visual Literacy (Grades 3-6)

The Language Support Manual expands this lesson by suggesting physical activities which help clarify the Comprehension Strategy Objective stated in the Teacher's Edition. This section also presents an opportunity to involve the ESL student with discussion prompts which explore the individual students cultural background and uses their prior knowledge to do a compare and contrast activity which will assist in introducing the lesson content.

*This section introduces the unit concepts and the vocabulary needed to understand them.*

## Vocabulary

Suggestions are given here for teaching the vocabulary strategies highlighted in the Teacher's Planning Guide. Notes may call attention to idioms, figurative language, or language special to the selection. The vocabulary words are included, together with questions and tips for helping children increase comprehension.

An example activity from the grade one lesson for *Sam's Song* follows:

> Invite children to play a game of "Find the Word." Organize the group into two teams. Write the vocabulary words on the board for both teams. Then invite one child from each team to the board and ask them to erase the word you call out. If a child erases the incorrect word, rewrite it. Play until one team erases all the words.

## Evaluate Prior Knowledge

Building background is particularly important when children's cultural diversity interferes with comprehension. It is equally important to bring the reading topic to life—give it some immediate relevance—when it is unfamiliar to those children.

**Recognize different prior knowledge bases; use familiar contexts to introduce unfamiliar topics.**

This section of the lesson includes activities to help children get to know something about the cultural traditions and beliefs that move the story along and that may influence characters' actions. It is important to remember that ESL children's prior knowledge bases were not developed around the cultural traditions of English. They need help developing strategies to activate their own prior knowledge, so crucial to constructing meaning. Recognize that it takes time to learn concepts using a familiar language, let alone a new one.

**Model the language and use props when possible.**

The activities in this section help ESL children deal with culturally unfamiliar topics by giving it a familiar context. The concept is brought to life as children are encouraged to draw upon their personal experience and knowledge to get the big picture. Role-playing, objects, story props, pictures, gestures, stories with practicable patterns, and story maps are used in many of the activities to help set the topic in a meaningful context.

The concept of learning something new is addressed in the grade one selection *Sam's Song.* An example from this section follows:

Ask children to name things they have recently learned to do or would like to learn to do. Write their responses on the chalkboard. Ask one child to work with you as you model teaching how to do one of the activities. For instance, you might help a child learn to tie her or his shoe.

Next invite children to work in pairs to learn something new from each other. They can learn something real, such as making a paper airplane, or pretend to learn something, such as how to drive a car.

## Develop Oral Language

In the grade one selection, *Sam's Song,* children build background by focusing on the concept learning something new. It is important to help children become active participants in learning and confident language users. The activities in this section offer opportunities for children to respond orally to activities more suited to their abilities.

This part of the lesson also offers suggestions for TPR commands you can use when teaching story concepts. Like their English-speaking classmates, ESL children will be at different levels of language and literacy proficiency in their native language. They will also be in various stages of English language acquisition.

## Guided Reading

**Preview, Predict, Read** In *Sam's Song,* children are guided through a picture walk of the book. As children are directed to look at the illustration, they are asked questions, such as: *What do Chuck, Mom, and Pop do under the moon? Who watches them sing? Why do you think Sam looks sad? What does Sam finally learn to do? How do you think he feels?* Based on the children's abilities, they are called on to give short answers.

**Graphic Organizer** A graphic organizer which follows each reading selection is designed to engage children in active learning. In the grade one selection, *Sam's Song,* a "Story Puppets" blackline master is available. Children are asked to color the pictures of Sam and his family and then cut them out. The pictures are glued to craft sticks and used as puppets. The children work in groups of four and use the puppets to act out the story as you reread *Sam's Song* aloud.

**Engage children in active learning.**

# Build Skills

**Blackline Masters**

This section contains directions for using the blackline masters as well as informal assessment suggestions.

## Phonics and Decoding (Grades 1-2)

This section of the Language Support lesson provides suggestions and activities to help children acquire phonics and decoding skills. Like other sections of the lesson, it follows the Teacher's Planning Guide materials, modifying them and adapting them where possible or providing alternative approaches to the skill that are more appropriate for second-language learners. It covers:

## Comprehension and Vocabulary Strategy

This section offers suggestions to help children develop comprehension and vocabulary skills throughout the selection. Lessons encourage you to ask simple questions that draw upon the children's own experiences, cultures, and ideas. The blackline masters give the students additional practice for each assessed skill introduced in the reading selection.

In the grade one selection, *Sam's Song,* the comprehension skill, Compare and Contract, is reviewed. Children are asked to use the story illustrations to help them find similarities and differences in the story. For example, children are directed to a page in the story, then asked: *Is Sam like the mouse? How is she different from the mouse?* Children then work in pairs to compare similarities and differences that they find.

## Informal Assessment

After each skill or strategy has been practiced with the blackline master the Language Support Manual includes an informal assessment activity which requires the students to return to the reading selection and apply the skill.

# ANN'S FIRST DAY pp. 12A–35R

Written by Constance Andrea Keremes Illustrated by Dorothy Donohue

## BUILD BACKGROUND FOR LANGUAGE SUPPORT

## I. FOCUS ON READING

### Focus on Skills

**OBJECTIVE:** Listen for short vowels *a, e, i, o, u*

**Alternate Teaching Strategy**
Teacher's Edition p. T64

**TPR**

### Develop Phonological Awareness

Read aloud the poem "Rabbit in the Rain." Say the word *hop* and model the action. Tell children that you will read the poem aloud again. Have children hop every time they hear a word that rhymes with *hop*. Ask children also to say aloud the rhyming word. Change the verse to explore other short vowel patterns. Say the word *tree* and stand with arms extended for tree branches. Have children stand like a tree and say the word that rhymes with *tree*. Do the same with *sun* (arms in a circle over their heads and say the rhyming word), and spin (spin around once and say the rhyming word).

## II. READ THE LITERATURE

**VOCABULARY**
hurry
shy
lucky
crawls
carrots
homework

### Vocabulary

Print the vocabulary words on the chalkboard. Assign small groups a different vocabulary word that they will act out. Using teaching chart 12, read the first sentence and point to the word *hurry*. Have a group demonstrate how they would hurry to catch the bus. Point to the word *shy* and have a group demonstrate being shy. Point to the word *lucky* and have a group demonstrate being lucky at a board game. Point to *crawl* and have a group show the class how a snake crawls. Point to *carrots* and have a group look through the story for pictures of carrots. Point to *homework* and have a group show the class the homework they have to do that night. Help children identify the words by sight, by pointing or approaching the chalkboard as groups complete their roleplays.

### Evaluate Prior Knowledge

**CONCEPT**
new places

Bring in an assortment of pictures or photos of places that are both familiar and unusual. For example, you might show pictures of a grocery store, library, park, swimming pool, principal's office, dentist's office, mountain top, space center, museum, the ocean, the Eiffel Tower, and so on. Have children tell if each picture is a place they have been before or if it is new to them. Then invite each child to choose one of the places they have never been to and act out what they would do there. Encourage them to demonstrate with their faces and actions how they might feel. Based on children's language proficiency, ask questions such as: *Which of these places have you visited? What do you do in each of these places? Who do you meet in each of these places? Which of these is your favorite place?*

## Develop Oral Language

nonverbal prompt for active participation

- Preproduction: *Show us* (Point to class and self.) *how you look* (show a variety of emotions on your face) *when you go to this new place.*

one- or two-word response prompt

- Early production: *What new place did you choose? Would you go there alone or with someone you know?*

prompt for short answers to higher-level thinking skills

- Speech emergence: *What is your place called? How would you feel when you went there for the first time? Why?*

prompt for detailed answers to higher-level thinking skills

- Intermediate fluency: *How do you feel when you go to new places? What kinds of things do you do to get ready for going to* (name the place the child chose)*?*

## Guided Reading

### Preview and Predict

Tell children that in this story Ann is starting a new school. Explain that she is also new in town and does not know any of the other boys and girls. Ask: *How do you think Ann feels about going to school?* Lead children on a picture walk using the story illustrations to reinforce the concept new places. Ask children to explain, name, or draw the emotions characters have in various illustrations. Ask questions such as: *Why is Ann afraid to start a new school? How does Ann spend her time when she is at home? What does Robbie do when Ann is gone? Why do you think the other children point to Ann's feet when she enters the classroom?*

### Objectives

**GRAPHIC ORGANIZER**
Blackline Master 1

- To reinforce comprehension of story characters
- To support hands-on learning
- To reinforce working together cooperatively

### Materials

One copy of Blackline Master 1 per child; pencils, crayons, or colored pencils; scissors; craft sticks; glue or paste; child copy of *Ann's First Day*

Invite children to color and cut out the characters from the Story Puppets page. Show children how to glue each figure onto a craft stick. Ann and Robbie are two-sided puppets. Ask children questions about the story, and have them respond by holding up the appropriate character. Ask questions such as: *Who is the new student in school? How does she feel about going to school? Who is the surprise visitor at Ann's new school? Who helps Ann when she feels shy?*

Have children use the story puppets to retell *Ann's First Day* to each other.

# III. BUILD SKILLS
## Phonics and Decoding

**SHORT VOWELS**
**_a, e, i, o, u_**
Blackline Master 2

**Alternate Teaching Strategy**
Teacher's Edition p. T64

**INFORMAL ASSESSMENT**

### Objectives
• To introduce short vowels _a, e, i, o, u_
• To blend and read short-vowel words

### Materials
One copy of Blackline Master 2 per child; crayons or colored pencils

Point to the first object in the row and say the word. With children, read the next two words in the row. Have children circle the word that has the same short-vowel sound as the first word.

Slowly recite a list of words. (run, not, pet, his, clap) Have children page through the story text to find and say each word.

## Phonics and Decoding

**REVIEW SHORT VOWELS**
**_a, e, i, o, u_**

Blackline Master 3

**Alternate Teaching Strategy**
Teacher's Edition p. T64

**INFORMAL ASSESSMENT**

### Objectives
• To review short vowels _a, e, i, o, u_

### Materials
One copy of Blackline Master 3 per child; crayons or colored pencils; scissors; glue or paste

Invite children to read the words at the top of the page aloud with you. Have children cut out the six words, match them to their corresponding pictures, and glue them in place.

Direct children to page 20. Ask them to identify an object in the picture containing a short _o_ as in _hop_. (box)

## Comprehension

**MAKING PREDICTIONS**
Blackline Master 4

**Alternate Teaching Strategy**
Teacher's Edition p. T66

**INFORMAL ASSESSMENT**

### Objectives
• To practice making predictions
• To support a hands-on approach to learning

### Materials
One copy of Blackline Master 4 per child; crayons or colored pencils

Invite children to describe what is happening in the top picture on their blackline masters. Ask children to think about what happened next in Ann's story, and invite them to draw their ideas in the box at the bottom of the page.

Show children page 25. Ask them to tell what happens next in the story. (Everyone laughs together and makes friends with Ann and Robbie.)

# Vocabulary Strategy

**INFLECTIONAL ENDINGS**
*-s, -es*
Blackline Master 5

**Alternate Teaching Strategy**
Teacher's Edition p. T67

## Objectives
• To introduce inflectional endings *-s, -es*
• To encourage varied reading and vocabulary strategies

## Materials
One copy of Blackline Master 5 per child; pencils, crayons, or colored pencils

Read the sentences aloud to children. Point to the picture to explain the pictured action. Then read the sentences aloud again, one by one. Have children use *-s* or *-es* to complete each verb. Then have them choose their own verb for the last sentence and write it on the line. Encourage children to illustrate their sentence in the space provided.

**INFORMAL ASSESSMENT**

Ask children to find and read a word on page 16 that ends in *-s* (runs, jumps, skips) and one that ends with *-es.* (marches)

# Story Puppets

# Read and Listen

**mom**

---

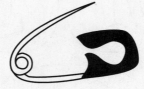

**fish**

---

**pet**

---

**sun**

---

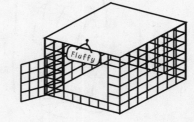

**clap**

# What's it Called?

| bag | bed | box |
|-----|-----|-----|
| pin | hug | wag |

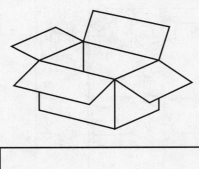

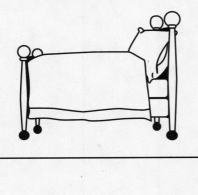

# What Next?

# How Does It End?

The hen sit _____ .

Ben miss _____ .

Sam wash _____ .

Ann fix _____ .

The cat nap _____ .

The bunny _____ .

# HENRY AND MUDGE pp. 36A–55R

Written by Cynthia Rylant  Pictures by Sucie Stevenson

## BUILD BACKGROUND FOR LANGUAGE SUPPORT

## I. FOCUS ON READING

### Focus on Skills

**OBJECTIVE:** Listen for long vowels *a, e, i, o, u*

**Alternate Teaching Strategy**
Teacher's Edition p. T68

**TPR**

### Develop Phonological Awareness

Read aloud "My Dog Jake" to children. Tell children to listen for the sound they hear in the middle of the word *Jake*. Emphasize the long *a* sound as children repeat it after you. Then name two objects in the classroom. One object should have the same long vowel sound as *Jake*. (face/fish) Invite children to point to and name the object with the same vowel sound. Repeat using the long vowel sounds for *i, o,* and *u*. You may wish to use the words *dime, globe,* and *cube*.

## II. READ THE LITERATURE

**VOCABULARY**
parents
worry
weighed
hundred
searched
different

### Vocabulary

Print the vocabulary words on the chalkboard. Demonstrate each word, and invite children to name the correct word.

*Parents:* Show pictures of families and ask a child to point to the parents. Say: *This man and woman are the parents.*

*Worry:* Show a worried look on your face. Say: *Oh dear, I hope it does not rain. What if my car breaks down! Did I remember to lock my door? I worry about many things.* Ask children to share what worries them.

*Weighed:* Use a balance scale to weigh a book. Say: *I just weighed this book.* Ask children how much they think they weigh.

*Hundred:* Write the numeral 100 on the board. Say: *This is one hundred.* Ask if any one in the room weighs more than 100 lbs? less than 100 lbs?

*Searched:* Pretend to look through a book bag or a desk. Say: *I have searched for my homework, but I can't find it.* Ask children to search for an object in the room which you will name.

*Different:* Show three books and one pencil. Say: *The pencil looks different from the books.* Ask children to show the class two things that are different.

### Evaluate Prior Knowledge

**CONCEPT**
pets as friends

Show children pictures of people with their pets, including images of the owner caring for the pet. Use a picture of yourself with a pet if possible.

Tell children they are going to create a pet show. Ask pairs of children to pretend to be a pet (dog, cat, fish, snake, hamster) and its owner. Tell children to think about what pets and their owners give each other and need from each other. Encourage children in the audience to clap when each pair completes its performance.

Take a walk through the school to visit any class pets. Tell other teachers of your interest and invite other children to show and tell about their class pets. Include class mascots, even if stuffed.

## Develop Oral Language

Tell children they are going on a visit to a pet store. Post pictures of different kinds of pets on the chalkboard. Ask children to make judgments about the pets based on their language proficiency.

**nonverbal prompt for active participation**

- Preproduction: Point to the pet you have or want to have. Model with your own photo or an example photo.

**one- or two-word response prompt**

- Early production: Which pet would you like to have? Can you tell me one thing you like about this pet?

**prompt for short answers to higher-level thinking skills**

- Speech emergence: What is this pet called? (Point to a pet.) Can you tell me more about this pet? What kinds of things could you do with this pet?

**prompt for detailed answers to higher-level thinking skills**

- Intermediate fluency: How would you take care of this pet? Tell us about a day with this pet.

# Guided Reading

## Preview and Predict

Tell children that in this story Henry has no brothers, sisters, or friends. He asks his parents for a dog. Ask: *How do you think Henry feels? Why might he want a dog?* Lead children on a picture walk using the story illustrations to review the concept of pets as friends. Ask children to predict how Henry feels at various points in the story. Point to the appropriate story picture, and have children respond by demonstrating Henry's emotion. Say: *Henry has no brothers, sisters, or friends on his block.* (Children should show sad faces.) *Henry's parents told him he could have a dog.* (Children show happy faces.) *What kind of dog do you think Henry would choose for a pet? How can you tell that Henry and his dog are friends?*

## Objectives

- To reinforce making predictions
- To reinforce working together cooperatively

**GRAPHIC ORGANIZER**
Blackline Master 6

## Materials

One copy of Blackline Master 6 per child; pencils; child copy of *Henry and Mudge*

**ALTERNATE TEACHING STRATEGY**
Teacher's Edition p. T66

Read aloud the first two pages of *Henry and Mudge*. Say: *Henry wants a dog.* Ask children if they think Henry's parents will let him have a dog. Explain that this guess is a prediction and point to the heading *Prediction* on the chart. Encourage children to use simple words or pictures to record their ideas in the *Prediction* column. Read aloud the next page to children. Ask children what actually happened when Henry asked for a dog. Have them record this information in the *What Happened* column. Encourage children to discuss with the class how their predictions matched what actually happened.

Reinforce the skill of making predictions. Ask pairs of children to tell how Henry will change after the story. Ask: *Will Henry stay smaller than Mudge?* (no)

# III. BUILD SKILLS

## Phonics and Decoding

**LONG VOWELS**
*a, e, i, o, u*
Blackline Master 7

**Alternate Teaching Strategy**
Teacher's Edition p. T68

### Objectives

- To review long vowels *a, e, i, o, u*
- To practice following verbal directions
- To match pictures showing words containing the same vowel sounds

### Materials

One copy of Blackline Master 7 per child; crayons or colored pencils

Invite children to examine the pictures at the top of the page and read aloud the words. Ask children to color each picture that corresponds with that word. Proceed to the next word, and follow the same directions with a different color. Continue until children have decorated each picture at the top of the page with a different color. Then ask children to look at the words at the bottom of the page. Ask children to say aloud the names of the objects at the bottom of the page. Have children color each object with the same long-vowel sound the same color as the object above .

**INFORMAL ASSESSMENT**

Page through the story text with children. Have them find and read words containing long vowel sounds.

## Phonics and Decoding

**REVIEW LONG VOWELS**
*a, e, i, o, u*
Blackline Master 8

**Alternate Teaching Strategy**
Teacher's Edition p. T72

### Objectives

- To review long vowels *a, e, i, o, u*
- To support hands-on learning
- To develop understanding of vowel patterns and consonant substitution

### Materials

One copy of Blackline Master 8 per child; scissors; pencils

Have children cut out the six squares at the top of the page. Use the square with the letter *m* to demonstrate how to create four words with the letters below. (mame, mice, mope, mune) Write these words on the board. Erase all nonsense words and explain that those remaining are real words. Invite children to create four new words using another letter square. Print these four words on the board and help children identify and erase the nonsense words. Encourage children to continue the activity with the remaining letter squares independently or with a partner.

**INFORMAL ASSESSMENT**

Point out to children the word *told* on story page 40. Have children cover the *t* with the word maker letter squares to create new words. Ask them to tell which words they recognize as real. (mold, fold)

# Comprehension

<table>
<tr>
<td>

**STORY ELEMENTS: PLOT AND CHARACTER**
Blackline Master 9


**Alternate Teaching Strategy**
Teacher's Edition p. T69

</td>
<td>

## Objectives
• To develop understanding of key story elements such as plot and character
• To support hands-on learning

## Materials
One copy of Blackline Master 9 per child; pencils, crayons, or colored pencils; child copy of *Henry and Mudge*

In the top box, ask children to draw a picture of the way Henry and Mudge looked at the beginning of the story. Show the first story page to clarify "beginning" if necessary. Help children review the story text for one or two words that describe what Henry thought about on the way to school. (ghosts, bullies) Then encourage children to draw a picture in the bottom box showing how Henry and Mudge looked at the end of the story. Discuss with children how Henry and Mudge have changed during the story.

</td>
</tr>
<tr>
<td>

**INFORMAL ASSESSMENT**

</td>
<td>

Have children work in mixed fluency teams to find text and illustrations describing and showing the ways Mudge changes. Ask children to read, point to, or draw the changes they can identify.

</td>
</tr>
</table>

# Vocabulary Strategy

<table>
<tr>
<td>

**INFLECTIONAL ENDINGS - *ed, -ing***
Blackline Master 10


**Alternate Teaching Strategy**
Teacher's Edition p. T67

</td>
<td>

## Objectives
• Review inflectional endings *-ed, -ing*
• To support hands-on learning
• To reinforce recognition of verbs and patterns for spelling them

## Materials
One copy of Blackline Master 10 per child; pencils

Review the page with children. Help them understand that the first part of the word is the root or base word, and the part they are adding is called the ending. Say: *When you put the word parts bark and -ing together, you get the word* barking. Ask children to circle the correct spelling of *barking*. Repeat for the remaining words on the page.

</td>
</tr>
<tr>
<td>

**INFORMAL ASSESSMENT**

</td>
<td>

Direct children to find action words in the story, such as *live* on page 50. Have children say and, if possible, write each word with the inflectional endings *-ed* and *-ing*.

</td>
</tr>
</table>

# What Will Happen?

| Predictions | What Happened |
| --- | --- |
|  |  |

# The Same Sounds

**cake**       **cheese**       **ice**

 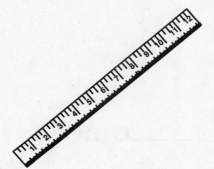

**hole**       **ruler**

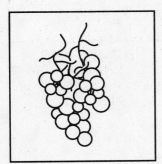 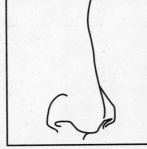  

   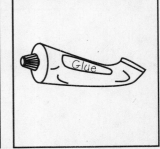

# What's it Called?
## Word Maker

| m | n | pr | r | sl | f |

_____ame

_____ice

_____ope

_____une

# A Change for Both

## At First

_____   _____

## At the End

_____   _____

# Word Math

_____

**1.** bark + ing = _____

**barking**          **barkking**

_____

**2.** like + ed = _____

**liked**          **likeed**

_____

**3.** hop + ed = _____

**hoped**          **hopped**

_____

**4.** run + ing = _____

**running**          **runing**

_____

**5.** jump + ed = _____

**jumpped**          **jumped**

_____

**6.** make + ing = _____

**makeing**          **making**

# LUKA'S QUILT pp. 56A–91R

Written and Illustrated by Georgia Guback

## BUILD BACKGROUND FOR LANGUAGE SUPPORT

# I. FOCUS ON READING

## Focus on Skills

### Develop Phonological Awareness

**OBJECTIVE:** Listen for long *a* and long *e*

Read aloud "The Green Field" several times to children. As you read, emphasize any words with long *a* and long *e* sounds. Then write the first four lines of the poem on the chalkboard. Invite children to help you make up a new, silly rhyme, substituting other long vowel *a* or *e* words in the blank spaces.

**Alternate Teaching Strategy**
Teacher's Edition p. T70

**TPR**

Grandma and I went out to _____. (wait, stay, read, see)

In a field we stopped to _____. (aim, pay, sleep, eat)

We sat beneath a green-leaf _____. (train, jay, peach, wheel)

Where we surprised a yellow _____! (brain, hay, flea, knee)

# II. READ THE LITERATURE

## Vocabulary

**VOCABULARY**
grandmother
idea
garden
remember
serious
answered

Print the vocabulary words on the board. Use the prompts below to help children understand the meaning of each word. Stop after each prompt and point to the word on the board. Say it and have children repeat it, before going on to the next one.

grandmother: Show a picture of a family with a child, a mother, and a grandmother. Point to the mother and say: *This is the child's mother.* Then point to the grandmother, say: *This is the mother's mother. And she is the child's grandmother.* Ask children to tell something about their grandmothers.

idea: Show a dull pencil, or one with a broken lead. Pantomime trying to figure out what to do about it. Say: *Hmmm. What should I do about this? Let me think. Oh, I have an idea! I'll sharpen it!* Have children repeat the word and give them opportunities to discuss ideas they have had.

garden: Ask a child to draw a picture of a flower on the chalkboard. Provide chalk in many colors. Then ask others, until all children have drawn a picture of a flower on the board. Say: *This is our flower garden.* Show pictures or photographs of real flower or vegetable gardens. Ask each child to come "pick" a flower from the garden on the board by erasing it. Have them say: *I picked a flower from the garden.*

remember: As children watch, draw a simple picture on the board, and then erase it. Say: *Who can remember what was on the board?* Ask children to respond by saying *I remember. It was a _____.*

serious: Pantomime doing something fun and show a happy face. Do the same with a sad face, a scared face, etc. Then say: *I have a lot to think about. I am very serious.* Have children show a serious face and repeat the word.

answered: Say to a child: *What's your name?* When the child says her or his name. Say: *Marco answered me.* Ask another child: *How old are you?* After the child answers, say: *Luisa answered me.* Let children work in small groups asking and answering each other's questions.

## Evaluate Prior Knowledge

Provide pictures or objects that represent crafts and traditions from various cultures. (Mexican piñata, Japanese origami, Irish-knit sweater, Ukrainian egg) Ask children to describe and, if possible, share or demonstrate crafts and traditions of their own culture. Give each child a chance to share. Then highlight any examples of cultural crafts or foods in the class or school environment. For example, visit the lunchroom and learn about cultural foods on the menu. Tour hallway bulletin boards or visit the art room for craft examples.

## Develop Oral Language

nonverbal prompt for active participation

Give each child a blank sheet of paper. With body language and a quilt illustration, explain that each child will decorate one square of a class quilt. Invite children to draw a picture that shows a cultural tradition or food she or he knows about. Tell children: *Draw something special to your family or culture. You might draw a special food, special day, or kind of clothing.* Help children arrange their papers to form a quilt, and tape the pieces together. Display the quilt on a board or wall. Prompt children to describe their quilt-square based on their language proficiency.

one- or two-word response prompt

prompt for short answers to higher-level thinking skills

prompt for detailed answers to higher-level thinking skills

• Preproduction: Point to the quilt. *Show us* (point to class) *your square.* Then model additional commands, such as *Point to your clothes or mouth to tell if this picture shows special food or clothing.*

• Early production: *What is this* (point to picture) *called? Tell us one word about it. Can you name who or what else is in your picture?*

• Speech emergence: *What is happening in the picture?* (point to picture) *What is this?* (point to specific element) *How is it used?*

• Intermediate fluency: *How do you feel when you (eat, celebrate, wear) this? How (why) do you do this?*

# Guided Reading

## Preview and Predict

Tell children that in this story, Luka and her grandmother make a quilt together. They also practice old traditions and make some new ones of their own. Lead children on a picture walk using the story illustrations to reinforce the concept of crafts and traditions. Ask children to pantomime what they can tell about the characters from looking at the pictures. Say: *Show me some things that Luka and her grandmother like to do together. Show me how Luka's grandmother feels when she gives her the quilt. How do you think Luka feels when her grandmother gives her the quilt?* Point to other pictures where you see Luka and her grandmother spending time together

## Objectives

GRAPHIC ORGANIZER
Blackline Master 11

• To reinforce understanding of story elements
• To analyze character and plot

## Materials

One copy of Blackline Master 11 per child; pencils; child copy of *Luka's Quilt*

Review the page with children. Point to Luka and Tutu and then to the *Character* heading. Tell children that Luka and Tutu make things happen in the story. For example, Tutu has a dream about a garden, and the dream inspires her to make a quilt. Have children follow along as you read aloud the text. Encourage them to think about what Luka and Tutu do or say that makes something else happen in the story. Invite children to draw a picture or write simple words about one of the characters in the first column and show how this affects the plot in the second column.

Reinforce understanding of plot and character. Have children retell the story from one of the character's point of view. Have them use the sentence frame: *When I _____ (didn't like the quilt), I _____ (told my grandmother).*

# III. BUILD SKILLS
## Phonics and Decoding

**LONG *a* AND LONG *e*: /a/ ai, ay; /e/ ee, ie, ea**
Blackline Master 12

**Alternate Teaching Strategy**
Teacher's Edition p. T70

**Objectives**
• To review long *a*: *ai, ay* and long *e*: *ee, ie, ea*
• To practice following verbal directions

**Materials**
One copy of Blackline Master 12 per child; crayons or colored pencils

Go over the page with children. Explain that they will circle the word that names the picture. Discuss each picture with children. Then read each word pair aloud. When children have circled their choices, check and correct their work. Then say: *Write the words you circled on the line below.*

**INFORMAL ASSESSMENT**
Write words from the story with long *a* and long *e* vowel sounds on the chalkboard. (dreamed, green, stay, plain) Ask children to find these words in the story text and then point to the picture on the page that has the same long-vowel sound pattern.

## Phonics and Decoding

**REVIEW LONG *a* AND LONG *e*: /a/ ai, ay; /e/ ee, ie, ea**
Blackline Master 13

**Alternate Teaching Strategy**
Teacher's Edition p. T70

**Objectives**
• To review long *a*: *ai, ay* and long *e*: *ee, ie, ea*
• To recognize and build words
• To support hands-on learning

**Materials**
One copy of Blackline Master 13 per child; scissors; glue or paste

Invite children to cut out the four letters at the top of the page. Demonstrate with *b* how each letter fits in only one box as the beginning sound for both words. Explain that the pictures offer clues to one of the word's meaning. Read the words aloud with children and help them determine the correct answers.

**INFORMAL ASSESSMENT**
Have children look at pages 64 and 65. Ask them to find in the illustrations one of the pictured words from the worksheet. Have children say the word aloud. (needle)

## Comprehension

**STORY ELEMENTS**
Blackline Master 14

**Alternate Teaching Strategy**
Teacher's Edition p. T69

**Objectives**
• To review story elements such as character and setting
• To emphasize the importance of setting in the story's meaning
• To support hands-on learning

### Materials

One copy of Blackline Master 14 per child; crayons or colored pencils; scissors; glue or paste

Invite children to color both pictures of Luka at the top of the page. As they are doing this, say: *Point to the picture that shows that Luka is happy. Point to the picture that shows that Luka is sad.* Ask children to cut out both pictures. Have them glue each picture to the setting that matches Luka's feelings in each setting—when her grand-mother presents Luka with the quilt, and at the Lei Day celebration.

**INFORMAL ASSESSMENT**

Show children pages 66–69. Ask: *Why was Luka sad when her grandmother showed her the quilt?* Then show pages 80–85. Ask: *Why was Luka happy at the Lei Day celebration?*

## Vocabulary Strategy

**CONTEXT CLUES**
Blackline Master 15

### Objectives
• To use pictures to determine the meaning of unfamiliar words
• To practice following directions

**Alternate Teaching Strategy**
Teacher's Edition p. T71

### Materials

One copy of Blackline Master 15 per child; scissors; glue or paste; crayons or colored pencils

Review the page with children. Use body language and words to explain that children should use picture clues to find meanings for the underlined words in the sentences. Invite children to cut out the four pictures at the top of the page. Help children read each sentence aloud and study its corresponding picture to define the underlined word. Tell children to glue the picture cutouts onto the appropriate picture. Have chil-dren color their page.

**INFORMAL ASSESSMENT**

Show children page 78. Ask them to use picture and text clues to define the word *blossom*.

Name _____ Date _____

# Charting Character and Plot

| Character | Plot |
|---|---|
| | |

# What's the Word?

**field**         **filed**

_____

_____

**reds**         **reads**

_____

_____

**pass**         **pays**

_____

_____

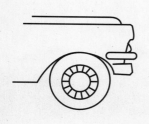

**while**         **wheel**

_____

_____

Grade 2

Name _____ Date _____

# What Else Do You See?

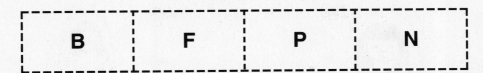

| B | F | P | N |

□ I E C E

A
I
L

□ E A N S

A
Y

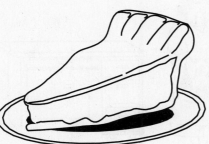

□ I E L D

E
E
T

□ A I L

E
E
D
L
E

Name _____ Date _____

# Where Was Luka?

---

---

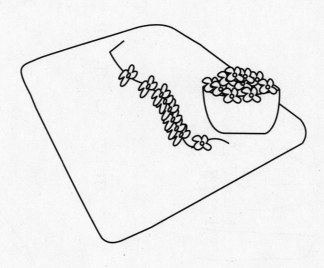

---

Grade 2

# What Belongs in the Picture?

**1.** Dad read a <u>magazine</u>.

**2.** I grew the <u>melon</u> myself.

**3.** Amy likes to play <u>basketball</u>.

**4.** She listened to a song on the <u>radio</u>.

# THE ROUNDUP AT RIO RANCH pp. 92A–113R

Written by Angela Shelf Medearis Illustrated by Karen Chandler

## BUILD BACKGROUND FOR LANGUAGE SUPPORT

## I. FOCUS ON READING

### Focus on Skills

**OBJECTIVE:** Listen for long *i* and long *o*

**Alternate Teaching Strategy**
Teacher's Edition p. T72

**TPR**
Invite children to walk around the classroom, pointing out objects whose names contain the /ī/ and /ō/ sounds. For example: *light, globe, poster.*

### Develop Phonological Awareness

Read aloud "My Goat Tom" to children. Explain that many of the words in the poem have the /ī/ and /ō/ sounds. Tell children to listen carefully as you slowly recite the poem again. Have children point to their eyes when they hear the long *i* sound. Have them make an "O" shape with their hands when they hear a long *o* sound.

## II. READ THE LITERATURE

**VOCABULARY**
cattle
broken
fence
carefully
safety
gently

### Vocabulary

Write the vocabulary words on the chalkboard. Say each word and have children repeat after you. Then tell children you are all going on a pretend ride around the ranch. Say: *First we must buckle our seat belts for <u>safety</u>.* Have them respond: *We buckle our seatbelts for safety.*

Then say: *Do you see all the <u>cattle</u>?* Have children point and respond: *We see the cattle.* Say: *Oh, no! I see a <u>broken</u> <u>fence</u>!* Ask if the children see it and have them say: *We see the broken fence, too!* Tell them you must stop and repair it. Give each child a pretend hammer and nail and say: *We must repair the fence <u>carefully</u>. How will you repair the fence?* Prompt them to respond with the word *carefully.* Pretend to hammer the fence and then say: *Look! Do you see the calf? Let's pet him <u>gently</u>. Show me how you would pet him gently.* Ask children to say: *We must pet the calf gently.*

**CONCEPT**
ranch life

### Evaluate Prior Knowledge

Use agricultural maps of Texas to show the areas where ranching is common. With props and drawings, try to convey the huge scale of the region and the numbers of cattle ranched. Invite any children with knowledge of Texas or cattle ranching to share their experiences.

Ask children what they think a *vaquero*, or *cowboy*, looks like. Show children photographs of modern ranchers and modern ranch life.

Invite children to work with a partner to create life-sized vaquero dolls. Have one child lay down on butcher paper, and have the other child trace her or him. Pairs should change places and repeat the process on a second piece of paper. Encourage children to decorate their life-sized paper dolls with clothing (hat, boots, chaps) and accessories (spurs, bandanna, lariat) that a vaquero (Spanish cowboy) would wear. Question children about their work according to their level of language proficiency.

## Develop Oral Language

Invite children to pantomime or demonstrate what a vaquero does. For example, pantomime riding a horse or throwing a lariat.

• Preproduction: *Show us* (point to self and class) *your vaquero. Point to the (hat, boots, bandanna).* Model responses: *She (He) is tall and has special boots.*

• Early production: *What is your vaquero wearing on her (his) (head, feet, neck)? Tell me one word about cowboys. Have you ever known a cowboy?*

• Speech emergence: *Describe what your vaquero is wearing. What do you know about cowboys and cattle ranching? Have you ever visited a cattle ranch? What was it like?*

• Intermediate fluency: *Why do you think vaqueros wear (a hat, boots, a bandanna)? Why is your vaquero dressed this way? What problems might a vaquero have without these special clothes?*

# Guided Reading

## Preview and Predict

Tell children that José is a young boy who lives on a ranch. He is going for the first time to help his father, grandfather, and brother round up their cattle. Lead children on a picture walk using the story illustrations to introduce characters and reinforce the concept ranch life. Encourage children to answer questions and prompts by pointing to the correct illustrations. Say: *What time of day is it in this picture? What kind of clothing is the boy wearing? How old do you think he is? Show us how you think he feels in this picture. What kind of animal is José riding? What does this animal "wear" to work? What do you think José does on his first roundup? Show us how you think Antonio feels at the end of the day.*

## Objectives
• To reinforce understanding of story elements
• To analyze character and setting
• To reinforce working together cooperatively

**GRAPHIC ORGANIZER**
Blackline Master 16

## Materials

One copy of Blackline Master 16 per child; crayons or colored pencils; scissors; craft sticks; paste or glue; child copy of *The Roundup at Rio Ranch*

Have children color and cut out their story puppet. Show them how to glue their puppet onto a craft stick. Invite children to work with a partner, and encourage them to retell the story to each other. Or, encourage children to use construction paper to create a setting for José and his horse. Have children color and cut out the story puppets and glue them onto the setting.

Reinforce the skill of Story Elements by having partners discuss and list everything they know about José and the place he lives and works. Ask pairs to share their lists with other children.

# III. BUILD SKILLS

## Phonics and Decoding

**REVIEW LONG *i* AND LONG *o***
Blackline Master 17

**Alternate Teaching Strategy**
Teacher's Edition p. T72

### Objectives
• To review long *i*: *i, y, igh* and long *o*: *o, oa, oe, ow*
• To decode and read words with long *i*: *i, y, igh* and long *o*: *o, oa, oe, ow*

### Materials
One copy of Blackline Master 17 per child; crayons or colored pencils; scissors; tag board; glue or paste

Review the page with children. Discuss the pictures and read aloud the words. Then invite children to color the pictures. Show them how to cut out the pictures, glue them onto a piece of tag board, and then glue each word card to the back of its corresponding picture. Encourage children to work with a partner to quiz each other or play a matching, sorting, or rhyming word game.

**INFORMAL ASSESSMENT**

Show children the illustration on page 104. Ask them to use a long *i* word from the worksheet to make a sentence telling where José is. (He is sitting *high* up on the horse.)

## Phonics and Decoding

**REVIEW LONG *i*: *i, y, igh* AND LONG *o*: *o, oa, oe, ow***
Blackline Master 18

**Alternate Teaching Strategy**
Teacher's Edition p. T66

### Objectives
• To review long *i*: *i, y, igh*
• To review long *o*: *o, oa, oe, ow*
• To practice following directions

### Materials
One copy of Blackline Master 18 per child; scissors; glue or paste

Go over the page with children. Review the pictures and invite ideas for what they show. Help children cut out the boxes at the top of the page. Explain that each letter or letters fits in only one of the boxes below to complete a word describing the picture. Help children sound out different words as they experiment with the various letter boxes.

**INFORMAL ASSESSMENT**

Direct children to the story text on page 99. Ask them to find a long *o* word. (rope) Have children say the word aloud and then point to a rope in the illustration.

## Comprehension

**REVIEW MAKE PREDICTIONS**
Blackline Master 19

**Alternate Teaching Strategy**
Teacher's Edition p. T66

### Objectives
• To make predictions
• To follow the sequence of events in a story
• To reinforce working together cooperatively

### Materials
One copy of Blackline Master 19 per child; crayons or colored pencils

Discuss the page with children, inviting them to tell what each picture shows. Then have pairs of children work together to explain the actions of the puppy. Urge children to point to the pictures on the page as they tell the story. Then have pairs brainstorm what might happen next and draw it in the last box. Invite children to explain their drawings to the class.

**INFORMAL ASSESSMENT**

Assess making predictions in small groups. Ask children to reread the last page of story text. *What do you think will happen next? Will José go on more cattle round-ups?* (Yes; he did a good job at this one.)

## Vocabulary Strategy

**CONTEXT CLUES**
Blackline Master 20

**Alternate Teaching Strategy**
Teacher's Edition p. T71

### Objectives
• To use pictures to determine the meaning of unfamiliar words
• To practice following directions

### Materials
One copy of Blackline Master 20 per child; scissors; glue or paste; colored pencils or markers

Go over the page with children. Read aloud and pantomime each sentence. Then ask children to describe what each picture shows. Invite children to cut out each sentence and glue it in the box that corresponds with the words. Review the choices children have made, and help them correct any misunderstandings. Children can then color their drawings.

**INFORMAL ASSESSMENT**

Show children the text and illustration on page 98. Ask children to use clues in both text and pictures to tell what the word *mustang* means. Prompt children by reading aloud the last paragraph on the page.

# Jose's Horse

Name _____ Date _____

# Picture-Word Cards

| high | cry | post |
|---|---|---|

|  |  | 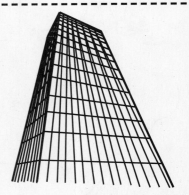 |

| hoe | road | blow |

| 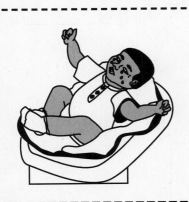 | 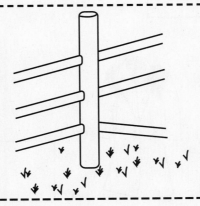 |  |

# Word Fill-ins

| igh | i | y | o | oa | ow | oe |
|-----|---|---|---|----|----|----|

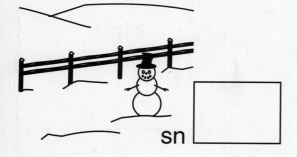

ch ▢ ld

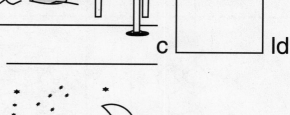

c ▢ ld

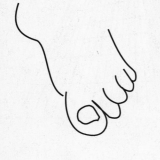 

t ▢

n ▢ t

sn ▢

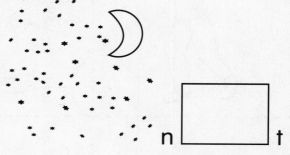

fl ▢

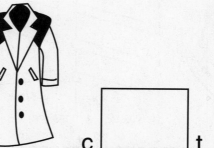

c ▢ t

# What Next, Pup?

# What Does it Mean?

| The cowboy looked into a deep <u>ravine</u>. | A cowboy sleeps in a <u>bunkhouse</u>. |
| The cows eat the grass in the <u>pasture</u>. | The cows drink from the <u>brook</u>. |

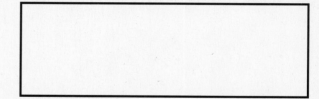

# WELCOME TO A NEW MUSEUM pp. 114A–123R

Time For Kids

## BUILD BACKGROUND FOR LANGUAGE SUPPORT

# I. FOCUS ON READING

## Focus on Skills

### Develop Phonological Awareness

**OBJECTIVE:** Listen for short and long vowels

**Alternate Teaching Strategy**
Teacher's Edition p. T64, T68

**TPR**
Have children listen to classmates say the rhymes. Invite children to stand when they hear the rhyming word.

Read aloud "When We Think of the Past" to children. Ask children to listen for the sound they hear in *tales*. Have children repeat the word with you. Then ask them to think of words that rhyme with *tales*. Prompt children with the following sentence frame: *When we think of tales, we think of whales*. Encourage children to supply additional words. After children name as many rhyming words as they can, repeat the activity using another word from the poem that has a long vowel sound. (snow, go; why, try) Then repeat using words from the poem that have short vowel sounds. (long, tell)

# II. READ THE LITERATURE

### Vocabulary

**VOCABULARY**
artist
visit
famous
body
life
hour

Print each vocabulary word on the chalkboard and say it aloud. Then assign children to stand in the following places as you present the words: *hour*, under the clock; *visit,* near the door; *body*, near another child; *artist,* near some art supplies; *famous,* near a classroom poster or supplied picture of a well-known personality; *life,* near simple biography books. Continue until all children are placed. Then include children of various fluency levels in pantomimes to explain each word.

### Evaluate Prior Knowledge

**CONCEPT**
museums

Explain to children that people might go to a museum to learn about art, animals, or the way other people live. Show children a display in your classroom or elsewhere in the school as an example. Discuss what is displayed and how it adds to viewers' knowledge. Invite children to share any experiences with the displayed items or with visiting museums. Then tell children that they are going to create a display that shows ways children their age live in different places. Use pictures of a school, homes, and a playground to help children choose from these topics: going to school, having fun, or time at home. Have children work together to paint pictures or collect objects that represent their topic. They may contribute items related to life in the United States or in another familiar place. Display children's work, and invite parents or another class to visit their exhibit.

### Develop Oral Language

Invite children to use actions or simple words to explain their display.

nonverbal prompt for active participation

- Preproduction: *Show us* (point to class and self) *how to use this* (name an object on display)

one- or two-word response prompt

- Early production: *What is this called* (point to an object on display)*? Do you think children in other places use this* (name an object on display)*?*

prompt for short answers to higher-level thinking skills

- Speech emergence: *When do children use this* (name an object on display)*? How do children use this* (name an object on display)*?*

prompt for detailed answers to higher-level thinking skills

- Intermediate fluency: *Why do you think children use this* (name an object on display)*? When have you used this* (name an object on display)*?*

## Guided Reading

### Preview and Predict

Tell children that people visit the museum described in this article to learn about important things that African Americans have done. Say: *Let's look at the pictures to see what we might find in this museum.* Then take children on a picture walk using the story illustrations to reinforce the concept of museums. Ask questions such as: *What do you think you might find in this museum? What do you think the flags are for on page 116? Look at the picture of the children and the picture of the statues. Do you see anything that looks the same? Look at the pictures on pages 118–119. What do you think these people are doing? Look at the map at the bottom of page 119. Where do you think this museum is located?*

**GRAPHIC ORGANIZER**
Blackline Master 21

### Objectives

- To reinforce making predictions
- To reinforce working together cooperatively

### Materials

One copy of Blackline Master 21 per child; pencil; child copy of *Welcome to a New Museum*

Pair an English-speaking child with one needing additional language support. Invite the language-proficient child to use the pictures to determine information such as a person, job, or event that she or he will learn about from reading the article. Have children record their predictions in the left column. Read aloud the article with children. Invite all children to record what they learned about their predictions in the right column. Children may use words or pictures as their fluency level determines. Encourage children to share their work with the class.

Invite pairs of children to tell each other predictions about a class visit to the Charles H. Wright Museum. What might children see, do, and learn?

# III. BUILD SKILLS

## Comprehension

**MAKING PREDICTIONS**
Blackline Master 22

**Alternate Teaching Strategy**
Teacher's Edition p. T66

**INFORMAL ASSESSMENT**

**Objectives**
• To reinforce making predictions
• To practice following directions

**Materials**
One copy of Blackline Master 22 per child; crayons or colored pencils

Prompt children to describe the scene at the top of the page. Invite children to decide what they think will happen next and draw a picture of it at the bottom of the page. Encourage children to color their drawings and share them with each other.

Reread "The Top Five" with children. Have them role-play a scene they predict could happen at one of the listed exhibits.

## Comprehension

**STORY ELEMENTS/
ANALYZE CHARACTER
AND SETTING**
Blackline Master 23

**Alternate Teaching Strategy**
Teacher's Edition p. T69

**INFORMAL ASSESSMENT**

**Objectives**
• To review story elements
• To practice following directions

**Materials**
One copy of Blackline Master 23 per child; crayons or colored pencils; scissors; glue or paste

Prompt children to name the three characters at the top of the page. Invite them to color the pictures, and then help them cut out the figures. Prompt children to describe the scene in each of the pictures below and have them decide which character belongs in each scene. Show children how to glue the character to the corresponding scene.

Return to Blackline Master 23 and display the pictures for children. Ask them to name setting details and tell how these affect the people shown.

## Vocabulary Strategy

**CONTEXT CLUES**
Blackline Master 24

**Alternate Teaching Strategy**
Teacher's Edition p. T71

**INFORMAL ASSESSMENT**

**Objectives**
• To review context clues
• To practice following directions

**Materials**
One copy of Blackline Master 24 per child; pencils; scissors; glue or paste

Read aloud each word at the top of the page with children. Then read aloud each sentence, and act it out. After each sentence, have children glue the word to the picture it matches.

Have children reread the sentence on page 117 containing *museum*. Ask them to use context clues in the surrounding text to build meaning for *museum*.

## INFLECTIONAL ENDINGS
### -s, -es
Blackline Master 25

### Alternate Teaching Strategy
Teacher's Edition p. T67

### INFORMAL ASSESSMENT

## Objectives
• To review inflectional endings -s, -es
• To practice following directions

## Materials
One copy of Blackline Master 25 per child; pencils

Prompt children to describe the action in each scene. Read aloud each sentence frame and pair of words. Have children circle the word that describes the action.

Say a word (rope, fish, flap) from the story, and have children add -s or -es to the word.

# What Will Happen?

| What We Will Learn at the Museum | What We Have Learned About the Museum |
| --- | --- |
|  |  |

Name _____ Date _____

# What Now?

# Who and Where?

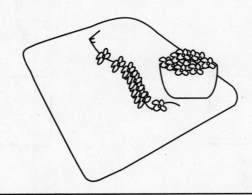

# You Can Figure it Out

| piano | shuttle | banner | clippers |

**1.** The man played the <u>piano</u>.

**2.** She flew through space in a <u>shuttle</u>.

**3.** A <u>banner</u> was flying over the roof.

**4.** People crossed the sea in <u>clippers</u> like this.

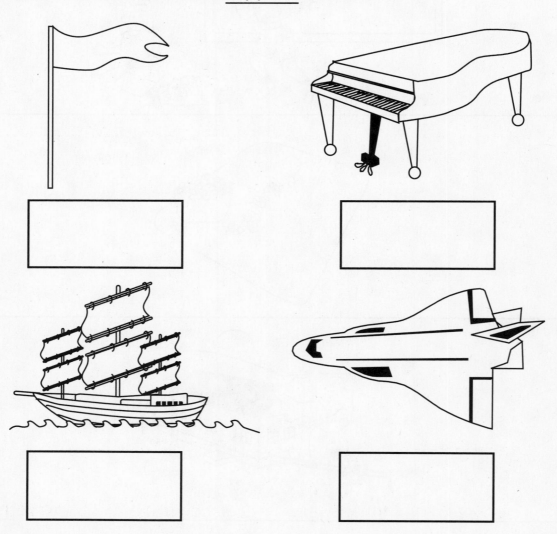

# A Lot to Do

**push**

The girl_____the door.

**pushs**     **pushes**

**spot**

She _____ the boat.

**spoted**     **spotted**

**look**

She _____ at it for a
long time.

**looks**     **lookes**

**move**

She is not _____.

**moving**     **moveing**

# LEMONADE FOR SALE pp. 128A–155R

Written by Stuart J. Murphy Illustrated by Tricia Tusa

## BUILD BACKGROUND FOR LANGUAGE SUPPORT

## I. FOCUS ON READING

### Focus on Skills

**OBJECTIVE:** Listen for /ü/

**Alternate Teaching Strategy**
Teacher's Edition p. T64

**TPR**

### Develop Phonological Awareness

Read aloud the poem "My Friends." Then say: *One, two, buckle my shoe. Tell me a word that sounds like Sue.* Reread the poem and ask children to stomp their feet when they hear words that contain the same vowel sound as Sue. Print the words on a piece of chart paper, and display it in the room. Read the first stanza of the poem leaving out the last word of each line. Ask children to think of another word with the /ü/ sound. Have them clap once as they say the new word in the last line of the stanza.

## II. READ THE LITERATURE

**VOCABULARY**
announced
empty
squeezed
poured
melted
wrong

### Vocabulary

Direct children to the illustrations in the story that show the vocabulary words *announced* (p. 138), *empty* (p. 133), and *squeezed* (p. 137). Ask children to draw the pictures from the illustrations on their own paper. On the chalkboard, draw a pitcher of water being poured into a glass, a puddle of water with an ice cube in the middle to show *melted*, and the letter *s* written in reverse to demonstrate *wrong*. Invite children to copy the chalkboard drawings. Tell children to cut out their pictures. Then model how to hold up the correct picture as you pantomime meanings and say the words aloud. Invite children to copy your pantomime as a classmate uses her or his pictures to "label" the pantomime.

### Evaluate Prior Knowledge

**CONCEPT**
fund-raising

Tell children that fund-raising means working together to earn money for a group to spend. Explain that schools, clubs, and teams often raise money by washing cars, selling food, or putting on a show. If possible, show pictures of or give examples from recent school or community fund-raisers. Invite children who have had fund-raising experience to share their knowledge with the class.

### Develop Oral Language

Encourage children to brainstorm ideas for fund-raising activities. Tell them to think about what services (car washing), foods, or entertainment (skits) they could sell. then model one idea with pictures and pantomime. Have children draw pictures and demonstrate their ideas. Question children according to their level of language proficiency.

**nonverbal prompt for active participation**

- Preproduction: *Show us* (point to self and class) *your picture.* (Model by holding a picture in front of you.) *Point to the* (name an object in the picture). *Show us your idea* (repeat your own pantomime to clarify). *Are you* (fill in appropriate description of activity)*?*

**one- or two-word response prompt**

- Early production: *Is this a picture of* (name the activity in the picture)*? What is one thing you need in order to* (name appropriate activity)*?*

**prompt for short answers to higher-level thinking skills**

- Speech emergence: *How many people do you need to* (point to picture or to demonstrating child)*? Do people need special tools or teaching to do this? What would you do with the money raised?*

**prompt for detailed answers to higher-level thinking skills**

- Intermediate fluency: *Tell us about your picture. Why do you think this is a good way to raise money? Will people want to buy this (service, food, entertainment)? What else do you know about fund-raising?*

## Guided Reading

### Preview and Predict

Tell students that the children in this story want to raise money to fix up their clubhouse. Read the title with children and then ask, *What do you think they did to raise money?* Lead children on a picture walk. Use the story illustrations to reinforce the concept of fund-raising. Ask: *How do you think the kids feel in this picture? How do you think they will use the bar graph shown here? What supplies do you think the kids need to make and sell lemonade? What work are they doing in this picture? Do you think the kids are selling a lot of lemonade? Why do you think people stopped buying the kids' lemonade? Do you think the kids will raise enough money to fix their clubhouse?*

### Objectives

**GRAPHIC ORGANIZER**
Blackline Master 26

- To reinforce the relationship between cause and effect
- To reinforce understanding of problems and solutions
- To reinforce working together cooperatively

### Materials

One copy of Blackline Master 26 per child; pencils; child copy of *Lemonade for Sale*

Remind children that the story characters did many things to solve their problems. Talk about how these actions cause something to happen in the story. As you read the story together, encourage children to record characters' actions in the left-hand column and the results in the right-hand column. Demonstrate one entry in each column, using a mixture of written and drawn entries. Pair less-fluent children with more advanced children.

To reinforce the skill of cause and effect, invite groups of children to role-play ac and results from the story.

# III. BUILD SKILLS
## Phonics and Decoding

**REVIEW /ü/: *oo, ue, ew***
Blackline Master 27

**Alternate Teaching Strategy**
Teacher's Edition p. T64

### Objectives
• To review /ü/: *oo, ue, ew*
• To review short *u*
• To practice following directions

### Materials
One copy of Blackline Master 27 per child; yellow and red crayons or colored pencils

Invite children to color the cup yellow and the newspaper red. Tell children they will be listening for words with the sounds they hear in the words cup and news. Read the word that the picture represents, beginning with the picture that represents glue. Ask children to decide whether they hear the /u/ in cup or the /ü/ in news. Tell children to color the picture in the box yellow if they hear a word that sounds like cup or red if they hear a word that sounds like news. Repeat with the remaining words.

**INFORMAL ASSESSMENT**

Say other /u/ words (luck, hut) and /ü/ words (tune). Then ask children to find words from the story. (glum, cup; Tuesday) Have children point to the picture of the cup or newspaper to identify the sound in each word.

## Phonics and Decoding

**REVIEW /ü/ *oo, ue, ew***
Blackline Master 28

**Alternate Teaching Strategy**
Teacher's Edition p. T64

### Objectives
• To review /ü/: *oo, ue*
• To blend and read /ü/
• To practice following directions

### Materials
One copy of Blackline Master 28 per child; crayons or colored pencils; scissors; glue or paste; tag board or cardboard

Invite children to color the pictures on the page. Tell them to color the ribbon blue. Help children cut out the strips with the pictures and glue them onto pieces of tag board or cardboard. Show them how to glue each word card to the back of its corresponding picture card. Encourage children to work with a partner to play a matching, sorting, or rhyming word game.

**INFORMAL ASSESSMENT**

Show children the first story page. Ask them to find an item in the picture that matches one of their cards. Have them hold up the card and say the word. (broom)

# Comprehension

**INTRODUCE PROBLEM AND SOLUTION**
Blackline Master 29

**Alternate Teaching Strategy**
Teacher's Edition p. T66

**INFORMAL ASSESSMENT**

## Objectives
• To identify problems and solutions in the story
• To practice following directions

## Materials
One copy of Blackline Master 29 per child; pencils

Go over the page with children. Discuss the story problems facing the characters. Invite children to draw a picture showing one of these problems in the left-hand column. Have children show how the characters solved this problem by drawing a picture in the right-hand column. Divide the class in half and have children on one side of the room act out the characters having a problem. Ask the other half to act out the solution.

Show children the first two story pages. Ask children to describe the characters' problem and tell how they solved it. (Their clubhouse is falling down and they need money to fix it. They sell lemonade to raise money.)

# Vocabulary Strategy

**INTRODUCE PREFIXES**
Blackline Master 30

**Alternate Teaching Strategy**
Teacher's Edition p. T67

**INFORMAL ASSESSMENT**

## Objectives
• To introduce the prefix *re-*
• To practice following directions

## Materials
One copy of Blackline Master 30 per child; pencils

Explain that putting *re-* in front of a word means something is done again. Then read the first word in each group together. Discuss the sequenced pictures and ask children to name the process. Tell them to write the new word on the line. If necessary, model putting *re-* in front of the first word on the chalkboard.

Read a word from the story such as *make* and show children the page on which it appears. (p. 134) Ask children to add *re-* to the word and say the new word. (remake) Have them tell you or demonstrate the meaning of the new word.

Name _____ Date _____

# What If We Sell Lemonade?

| Cause | Effect |
|---|---|
| | |

# You Choose

cup —

news

Name _____ Date _____

# Picture-Word Cards

| glue | blue | stew |
|---|---|---|

| broom | school | dew |
|---|---|---|

Name _____ Date _____

# What a Problem!

**Problems**

**Solutions**

# Again!

**write**

re _____

**build**

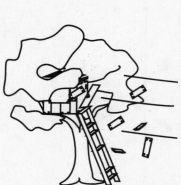

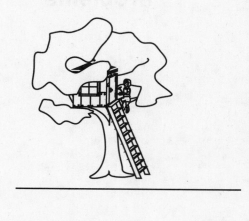

re _____

**enter**

re _____

# A LETTER TO AMY pp. 169A–191R

Written and Illustrated by Ezra Jack Keats

## BUILD BACKGROUND FOR LANGUAGE SUPPORT

## I. FOCUS ON READING

### Focus on Skills

**OBJECTIVE:** Listen for /ou/ and /oi/

**Alternate Teaching Strategy**
Teacher's Edition p. T68

**TPR**

### Develop Phonological Awareness

Read aloud "The Lost and Found Kite." Say the /ou/ sound. Have children repeat the sound with you. Say: *You hear the* /ou/ *sound in words such as sound and ground.* Then say the /oi/ sound and have children repeat it. Say: *You hear the* /oi/ *sound in words such as* Roy *and* boy. Read aloud the poem again, and ask children to touch the ground every time they hear a word that has the /ou/ sound. They should point to any boy in the class when they hear a word that has the /ou/ sound.

## II. READ THE LITERATURE

**VOCABULARY**
special
corner
glanced
wild
repeated
candles

### Vocabulary

Use these suggested activities to make sure children understand the meaning of the following vocabulary words.

Special: Show children things that are special to you such as a birthday card, a picture of your family, a diploma, a piece of jewelry. Explain why it means so much to you.

Corner: Stand in the corner of the room; point to a corner of a desk, touch the corner of a book.

Glanced: Look quickly at something and then look away.

Wild: Show pictures from a magazine or encyclopedia of a house cat and a wild cat, such as a tiger or lion. Demonstrate the behavior of a tame cat by walking around slowly and calmly. Then act like a wild cat by snarling and leaping. Invite children to do the same.

Repeated: Ask the same question or read a statement over and over.

Candles: Show a candle or a picture of candles on a cake.

Tell children that they're going to help you write an invitation for a pretend birthday party. Ask how each of the vocabulary words may be used in the invitation. As they use each one, circle the word, or write it in a different color chalk.

**CONCEPT**
special events

## Evaluate Prior Knowledge

Use wrapping paper to cover a box containing a typical party object. (balloon, hat, tiny present, candy) Invite children to make guesses about the contents of the box by asking "yes or no" questions. (Is it red? Can you eat it? Does it make a sound?) Have children unwrap the "gift" when they correctly guess the name of the object.

Bring in an assortment of greeting cards for different occasions such as birthday, congratulations, and baby shower cards. Select those with pictures that clearly portray the occasion. Show children the cards and have them draw or tell what the occasion is, who might give the card, and who might receive the card. Invite children to discuss how each card shows a special event.

## Develop Oral Language

Tell children they are going to share the fun of a party with the class. Ask each child to demonstrate something they enjoy about parties. They can create props, such as drawings of food, if they wish. After each child has presented her or his favorite thing to do at a party, encourage them to work together to make a list of things they would like for a real class party. As children demonstrate their favorite party activities, ask them questions, according to their level of language proficiency

nonverbal prompt for active participation

- Preproduction: *Show us* (point to class and self) *you* (point to child) *at a party.* Help children describe themselves. Say: *You are (dancing, eating, singing). You look happy*

one- or two-word response prompt

- Early production: *Do you like parties? What do you like to eat at a party? Who do you want to come to a party?*

prompt for short answers to higher-level thinking skills

- Speech emergence: *What are you doing at your party? What is the party for? When did you have this kind of party?*

prompt for detailed answers to higher-level thinking skills

- Intermediate fluency: *What else do you like about parties? Is there anything you don't like about parties? How do you get ready for a party? How do you tell others about the party?*

# Guided Reading

## Preview and Predict

Tell children that Peter wants his friend Amy to be part of a special day in his life. Ask: *How do you think Peter feels about Amy?* Take children on a picture walk, and point out illustrations to clarify characters and support the concept of special events. Encourage children to point to the picture that answers the following questions. Ask: *How does Peter invite Amy to his party? What has Peter done to dress for a rainy day? What problems does the weather cause for Peter? Why doesn't Peter want Amy to see the letter before he mails it? Why might Peter think that Amy is mad at him? How do we know that Amy isn't mad at Peter? Do you think Peter will have a happy birthday?*

**GRAPHIC ORGANIZER**
Blackline Master 31

## Objectives

- To reinforce understanding of problems and solutions
- To reinforce working together cooperatively

**Alternate Teaching Strategy**
Teacher's Edition p. T66

**Materials**

One copy of Blackline Master 31 per child; pencils; child copy of *Letter for Amy*

Tell children that Peter has some problems that might ruin his birthday party. Use story illustrations or classroom examples to demonstrate problems and solutions. Encourage pairs of children to identify a problem Peter had in the story. Model by saying: *Peter had a problem. He forgot to write the day and time on the party invitation. He solved the problem by writing it on the envelope.* Have pairs of children write the problem in the left-hand column, and the solution in the right-hand column. Ask children to look for and record other problems and solutions in the story as you go through together.

To reinforce the skill, invite pairs of children to pantomime their problem and solution for the class.

# III. BUILD SKILLS
## Phonics and Decoding

**DIPHTHONGS /ou/ *ow, ou;* /oi/ *oi, oy***

Blackline Master 32

**Alternate Teaching Strategy**
Teacher's Edition p. T68

**Objectives**
• To review words with /ou/ *ow, ou* and /oi/ *oi, oy*
• To blend and read words with /ou/ *ow, ou* and /oi/ *oi, oy*

**Materials**
One copy of Blackline Master 32 per child; scissors; paste or glue

Look at each picture with the children and have them discuss what they see. Read the words at the top of the page and have children repeat them after you.  Have children match the word to the corresponding picture and glue it in place. Allow children to choose a word to demonstrate for the rest of the class. Model what you want them to do by saying: *I'm so sad. What do you see on my face?*

**INFORMAL ASSESSMENT**

Display story pages 170–171. Ask children to find in the text or illustrations a word containing /ou/ *ou*. (cloud)

## Phonics and Decoding

**REVIEW /ou/ *ow, ou;* /oi/ *oi, oy;* /ü/ *ew***

Blackline Master 33

**Alternate Teaching Strategy**
Teacher's Edition p. T68

**Objectives**
• To review /ou/ *ow, ou* ; /oi/ *oi, oy;* /ü/ *ew*
• To work cooperatively

**Materials**
One copy of Blackline Master 33 per child; crayons or colored pencils; scissors

Read aloud to children the first six words. Emphasize the diphthong in each. Read aloud each of the next six words. Pause after each word to demonstrate its meaning. Then have children draw a picture of the word. After children have drawn a picture for each word, help them cut out the 12 cards. Have children work in pairs to say aloud and then match the cards that have the same sound.

**INFORMAL ASSESSMENT**

Pair children for assessment. Refer partners to story text on page 171. Have children find a word on the page with the diphthong /oi/ *oi*. (spoiled)

# Comprehension

| | |
|---|---|
| **INTRODUCE MAKE INFERENCES**<br>Blackline Master 34 | **Objectives**<br>• To make and explain inferences<br>• To practice following directions<br>• To extend the story |
| **Alternate Teaching Strategy**<br>Teacher's Edition p. T69 | **Materials**<br>One copy of Blackline Master 34 per child; pencils; crayons or markers<br><br>Say: *This girl is dressed to go outside. What kind of day do you think it is outside?* Invite children to draw a picture in the window showing the kind of weather they think is outside the girl's house. Have children exchange pictures and explain their reasons to another child. |
| **INFORMAL ASSESSMENT** | Have children look at the story illustrations on page 162–163. Ask children what kind of weather they think Peter is planning for. (rain) Have children point to clues in the picture that helped them infer. (Peter's clothes) |

# Vocabulary Strategy

| | |
|---|---|
| **INTRODUCE COMPOUND WORDS**<br>Blackline Master 35 | **Objectives**<br>• To read and use compound words<br>• To practice following directions |
| **Alternate Teaching Strategy**<br>Teacher's Edition p. T71 | **Materials**<br>One copy of Blackline Master 35 per child; pencils<br><br>Review the page with children. Use classroom objects to create a compound word equation and explain the concept to children. Read aloud a word from the workbook page. Then read the first half of the word, point to its picture, and invite children to cross out that picture. Repeat the process with the second half of the word. Read the whole word again, and have children circle the remaining picture to represent the compound word. |
| **INFORMAL ASSESSMENT** | Refer children to story text page 162. Ask them to find the compound word on the page and then on the worksheet. (raincoat) |

Name _____ Date _____

# What's the Problem?

## Peter

| Problem | Solution |
|---|---|
|  |  |

# Picture-Word Cards

| clown | joy | cloud |
|---|---|---|
| frown | point | cow |

# You Draw It!

| | | |
|---|---|---|
| 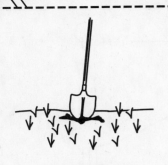<br>**soil** | <br>**joy** | <br>**town** |
| <br>**blouse** | <br>**spoon** | <br>**shoot** |
| **mouse** | **crown** | **toy** |
| **boot** | **oil** | **moon** |

# What's It Like Out There?

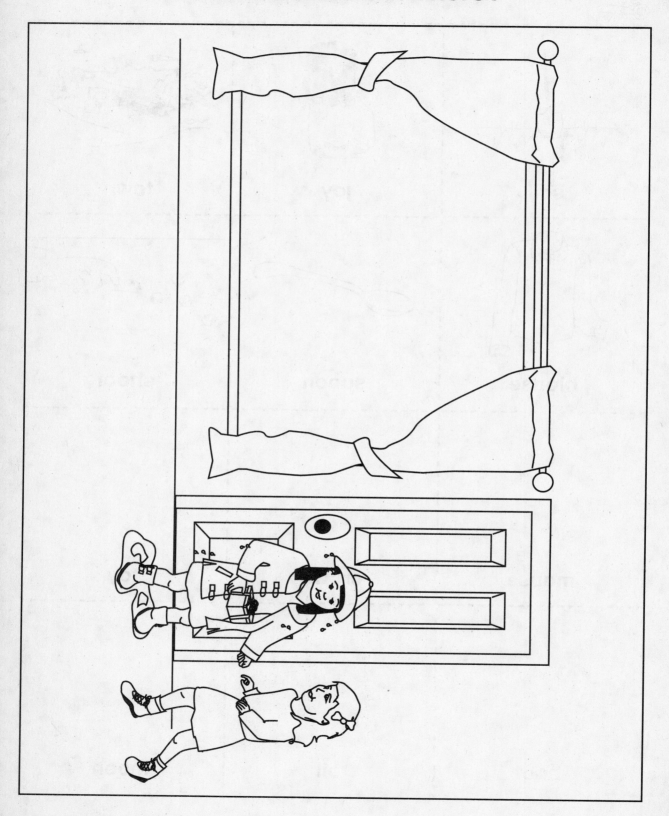

# Find the Right Picture

**mailbox**

**doorbell**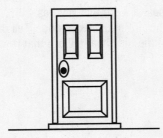

**cupcake**

**meatball**

**raincoat**

# THE BEST FRIENDS CLUB pp. 192A–215R

Written by Elizabeth Winthrop Illustrated by Martha Weston

## BUILD BACKGROUND FOR LANGUAGE SUPPORT

## I. FOCUS ON READING

### Focus on Skills

**OBJECTIVE:** Listen for *r*-controlled vowels: /âr/: *are,* /ôr/: *or, ore,* /îr/: *ear*

**Alternate Teaching Strategy**
Teacher's Edition p. T70

**TPR**

### Develop Phonological Awareness

Show children a picture of a hare. Then say the word *hare,* emphasizing the sound /ar/. Explain that a hare is a type of rabbit. Tell children that you are going to read aloud the poem "Surprise for Tim." Ask children to act like hares (holding fingers up for ears) every time they hear a word that rhymes with *hare.* Repeat the activity, this time emphasizing the sound /ôr/ in the word door. Tell children to pretend they're knocking on a door every time they hear a word that rhymes with *door.*

## II. READ THE LITERATURE

**VOCABULARY**
president
allowed
rule
leaned
whispered
promise

### Vocabulary

Print the vocabulary words on the chalkboard. Then read aloud from the story sentences containing vocabulary words. Invite children to guess the meaning of each vocabulary word, based on clues in the sentence. Do the following activities to further develop vocabulary:

*whispered:* Whisper to the class: *Hello, my name is_____.* Ask children to whisper to each other and then tell you who they whispered to. For example, *I whispered to Carlo.*

*leaned:* Lean against the wall and say: *I leaned against the wall.* Invite children to lean against something and then say what they did.

*president:* Show a picture of the president of the United States and say: *This is our president. He is the leader of our country.*

*rule:* Ask the class to help you create a list of school rules on the chalkboard.

*allowed:* Use the list of rules and ask a question such as: *Are we allowed to run in the hall?* Have children respond: *We are not allowed to run in the hall.*

*promise:* Refer to the list of school rules and say: *Do you promise to follow the school rules?* Have children respond: *I promise to follow the school rules.* Ask: *What happens if you don't keep your promise?*

### Evaluate Prior Knowledge

**CONCEPT**
clubs

Bring in any materials (membership cards, patches, hats, T-shirts, rulebooks, and so on) associated with clubs. If appropriate, tell and show children about clubs to which you belong.

Bring in pictures of two or more people participating in a group or team activity. (scouting, soccer, computers, reading) Say: *Sometimes people form a group called a club to share an activity they all enjoy. They make rules and have jobs that help the club in different ways.*

## Develop Oral Language

Talk about the many kinds of clubs people form. Explain that some clubs work to help other people (new students, older neighbors) or the environment (clean up the park). Give each child a sheet of paper. Encourage them to think of such a club and then draw a symbol that represents its goal. Ask children to share their drawings with the rest of the class. Organize different clubs based on the children's ideas. Make posters to show the kind of club. Then invite children to join a club that interests them and allow those small groups to meet to enjoy their club's focus. Encourage groups to create a sign, choose a president, and make rules for their club. Ask each group to present its club to the class.

nonverbal prompt for active participation

- Preproduction: *Show us your* (point to the picture). *Show us* (point to self and class) *who your club helps.*

one- or two-word response prompt

- Early production: *Do you belong to a club like this one? Would you like to? Can anyone join your club? Can you show or tell us one thing people in your club do?*

prompt for short answers to higher-level thinking skills

- Speech emergence: *What rules does or should your club have? What materials might you need? What kinds of people do you need in your club?*

prompt for detailed answers to higher-level thinking skills

- Intermediate fluency: *How can you get people to join your club? Would you like to be the club's leader? Why or why not?*

# Guided Reading

## Preview and Predict

Tell children that Lizzie and Harold are best friends. Explain that they form a club, but start having problems when Lizzie makes too many rules. Take children on a picture walk. Point out illustrations that identify the characters and support the concept of clubs. Ask questions such as: *What do you think Lizzie and Harold do with the signs they make? What else are they making? Where does their club meet? Who makes the rules? How does Lizzie feel when she sees Harold walking home with Douglas?*

## Objectives

**GRAPHIC ORGANIZER**
Blackline Master 36

- To reinforce making and explaining inferences
- To reinforce working together cooperatively
- To develop critical thinking skills

**Alternate Teaching Strategy**
Teacher's Edition p. T69

## Materials

One copy of Blackline Master 36 per child; scissors; crayons or colored pencils; child copy of *The Best Friends Club*

Invite children to color and cut out the three masks. Organize children in small groups. Ask children to take turns holding up one of the masks to her or his face. Then have other group members tell which character their classmate is. Ask children to use clues on the mask to support their choices. Mask-wearers may also try to act like the story character they believe their mask represents.

To reinforce the skill of making inferences, have trios of children role-play a story. Have other children tell how the characters feel during the scene.

# III. BUILD SKILLS
## Phonics and Decoding

**REVIEW** /âr/ *are*; /ôr/ *or, ore*; /îr/ *ear*
Blackline Master 37

**Alternate Teaching Strategy**
Teacher's Edition p. T70

### Objectives
• To listen for *r*-controlled vowels: /âr/ *are*; /ôr/ *or, ore*; /îr/ *ear*
• To practice following directions
• To expand phonemic awareness by matching pictures to words

### Materials
One copy of Blackline Master 37 per child; pencils

Review the page with children. Discuss and define together each pictured work. Prompt children to use the words *fork, store, hear, tears,* and *scare* to label the pictures on the page. Then read aloud the word alternatives. Tell children to listen for the sounds heard in *care, or,* or *ear.* Encourage children to then circle the word that contains one of these sounds and describes the corresponding picture.

**INFORMAL ASSESSMENT**

Assess children in pairs or small groups. Have pairs of children find at least two /âr/, /ôr/, or /îr/ words in the story text. (shared, porch, heard, four, pairs, etc.) Ask pairs to say the words aloud and sort them by vowel sound.

## Phonics and Decoding

**CUMULATIVE REVIEW**
Blackline Master 38

**Alternate Teaching Strategy**
Teacher's Edition pp. T68, T70

### Objectives
• To review /âr/, /ôr/, /îr/
• To review diphthongs /ou/ *ow, ou*; /oi/ *oy*
• To review variant vowel /ü/ *oo, ew*

### Materials
One copy of Blackline Master 38 per pair of children; crayons or colored pencils in at least three different colors; scissors

Invite children to work with a partner. Tell children to color the letters *-oon* and the four letters below (m, sp, s, n) one color. Have children color the letters *-ow* and the five letters below (b, c, h, n, w) another color. Tell children to color the letters *-ore* and the six letters below (c, ch, m, sh, st, t) a third color. Ask children to cut out all of the letters and arrange them in three piles according to color. Invite children to work with one pile of letters at a time to create as many words as they can. Encourage children to record their words on a sheet of paper. Have children repeat the procedure with the remaining two piles.

**INFORMAL ASSESSMENT**

Direct children to story page 201. Have them find and say the text word that also appears on the worksheet. (more) Then write a sentence about Lizzie: *Soon Lizzie will forget how to be friends.* Ask children to use the word-maker to make and show the underlined words. Have children say all three words.

# Comprehension

**REVIEW PROBLEMS AND SOLUTIONS**
Blackline Master 39

**Alternate Teaching Strategy**
Teacher's Edition p. T66

**Objectives**
• To review identifying problems and solutions
• To practice following directions

**Materials**
One copy of Blackline Master 39 per pair of children; pencils; crayons or colored pencils; scissors

Invite children to work with a partner. Write the words *Problem* and *Solution* on the board. Draw a vertical line separating the two. Invite children to cut out the pictures on the page. Have children choose pairs of pictures that show a problem and a solution. Invite volunteers to hold their *problem* and *solution* pictures in the correct columns on the chalkboard. Repeat the procedures with the second *problem* and *solution* pair. Then have children draw their own solution to the final problem.

**INFORMAL ASSESSMENT**

Using the text and illustration on page 205, have children tell about Lizzie's problem. Then ask pairs to draw or tell about a possible solution.

# Vocabulary Strategy

**REVIEW PREFIXES *re-*
AND *un-***
Blackline Master 40

**Alternate Teaching Strategy**
Teacher's Edition p. T67

**Objectives**
• To review prefixes *re-* and *un-*
• To practice following directions

**Materials**
One copy of Blackline Master 40 per child; pencils

Remind children that the prefix *re-* means "again" and the prefix *un-* means "not." Read the word under the first picture aloud. Then say: *Make a new word by adding the letters re- or un- to the word.* Then discuss what the other pictures show. Have children read aloud the remaining words with you, first alone and then with *re-* and *un-* before them. Tell children to decide which prefix to use to create a word that describes the picture. Ask children to write the new word under the picture.

**INFORMAL ASSESSMENT**

Show children story page 196 and point out the word write. Have children show or tell you what the word means. Then ask them to add *re-* or *un-* to the word. Ask: *Which makes a word?* (rewrite) Have children find a story page on which Lizzie rewrites the club sign.

# Funny Face

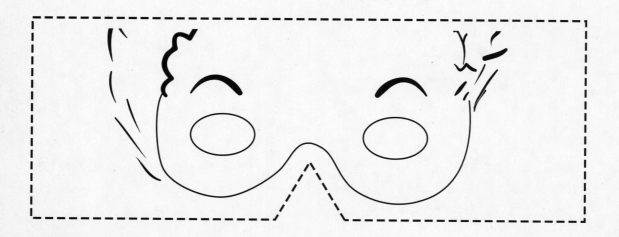

Grade 2

Name _____ Date _____

# Sights and Sounds

1.     **fork**     **fare**     **fear**

2.     **stare**     **store**     **steer**

3.     **hare**     **horse**     **hear**

4.     **tore**     **tears**     **tarts**

5.     **score**     **scare**     **sorts**

© McGraw-Hill School Division

# Word Maker

| oon | ow | ore |
|-----|-----|-----|
| m | b | c |
| sp | c | ch |
| s | h | m |
| n | n | sh |
|  | w | st |
|  |  | t |

# What's the Answer?

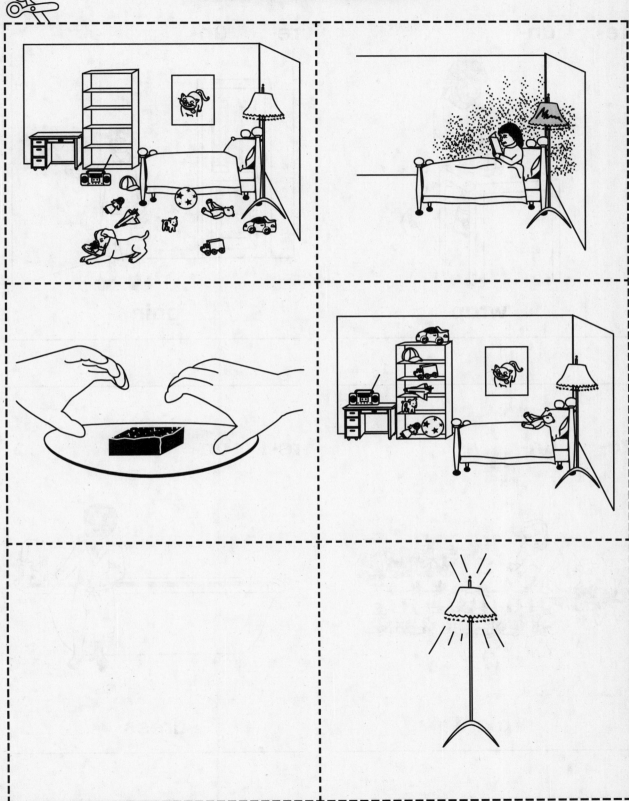

# Redo or Undo?

re-    un-

**wrap**

_____

_____

re-    un-

**paint**

_____

_____

re-    un-

**plant**

_____

_____

re-    un-

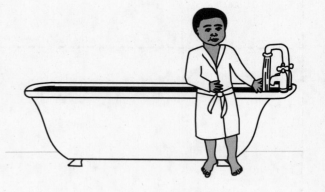

**dress**

_____

_____

# JAMAICA TAG-ALONG pp. 216A–243R

Written by Juanita Havill  Illustrated by Anne Sibley O'Brien

## BUILD BACKGROUND FOR LANGUAGE SUPPORT

## I. FOCUS ON READING
### Focus on Skills

**OBJECTIVE:** Listen for *r*-Controlled Vowels /är/ and /ûr/

**Alternate Teaching Strategy**
Teacher's Edition p. T72

**TPR**

### Develop Phonological Awareness

Read aloud "Arthur, Arthur". Emphasize the /är/ sound in *cellar* and the /ûr/ sound in *skirt* and *purse*. Have children repeat these sounds after you. Then say the following words slowly, in random order. Tell children to raise their arm if they hear the /är/ sound, or pretend they are digging in dirt if they hear the /ûr/ sound.

| cart | burn | fur | chart | fern | stir | smart |
| shirt | swerve | first | harm | curl | her | farm |

## II. READ THE LITERATURE

**VOCABULARY**
repair
giant
busy
form
edge
building

**CONCEPT**
being a younger child

### Vocabulary

Print the words on the board. Give children blocks. Invite them to follow your directions to use the blocks. Point to the words when appropriate and have children look at the word on the board, and repeat the word in context. Say: *Form a tower out of blocks and knock it down. Now, repair your tower.* (Demonstrate how to rebuild the tower.) *Build a giant tower.* (Continue adding blocks to your tower.) *This is the edge of a block.* (Point to the edge of a block.) *She (he) is building a tower.* (Point to a child.)

### Evaluate Prior Knowledge

Ask children to name other children in their families. Use drawings to clarify the concept of age position in the family. Then ask children to explain their own position in the family. If children in the class have siblings in the school, work together to identify them by name and class. Ask children to name something they do with their sibling, or would like to do with a sibling.

### Develop Oral Language

Ask children to role-play or pantomime a recent experience with a sister or brother; in the case of children who have no siblings, ask them to act out an experience with an imaginary sibling. Adjust the following questions accordingly.

<table>
<tr><td>nonverbal prompt for active participation</td><td>• Preproduction: Show us (point to class and self) what you (point to the child) did with your sister (brother).</td></tr>
<tr><td>one- or two-word response prompt</td><td>• Early production: What is your sister's (brother's) name? Can you tell me one thing about your sister or brother? Who is older? Do you like doing things with your sister or brother?</td></tr>
<tr><td>prompt for short answers to higher-level thinking skills</td><td>• Speech emergence: What is your sister (brother) doing in the activity you showed us? What are you doing? How do you feel about the activity? How do you think your sister (brother) feels about the activity?</td></tr>
<tr><td>prompt for detailed answers to higher-level thinking skills</td><td>• Intermediate fluency: Tell us how you feel about your sister (brother).</td></tr>
</table>

## Guided Reading

### Preview and Predict

Tell children that in this story they are about to read, big brother Ossie doesn't like it when Jamaica tries to tag-along with him. Jamaica feels hurt and doesn't understand Ossie's feelings until she meets a child younger than herself, who also wants to "tag along." Point out the characters in the illustrations and ask questions to explore the concept of being the younger child: *What is Ossie planning to play? What might Jamaica be asking Ossie? Do you think Ossie is happy about Jamaica coming to play? Where does Jamaica go? Who does Jamaica meet there? Who is playing together at the end of the story?*

### Objectives

**GRAPHIC ORGANIZER**
Blackline Master 41

• To explore problems and solutions
• To reinforce working together cooperatively

**Alternate Teaching Strategy**
Teacher's Edition p. T66

### Materials

One copy of Blackline Master 41 per child; scissors; crayons or colored pencils; child copy of *Jamaica Tag-Along*

Review the problem and solution chart with children. Model a simple classroom problem and solution to clarify the relationship and the chart headings. For example, you might say, *We have three books and four children want to read them. What is the problem? How might we solve the problem?* Then invite children to work in pairs to role-play either Jamaica's or Ossie's part of the story. Encourage children to discuss the problems Jamaica faces and how she solves them. After children explore each problem and solution, have them write or draw their ideas on the page.

To reinforce the skill of problem and solution, have children prompt each other by naming one problem from the story that is similar to something they have experienced. Invite partners to share solutions.

# III. BUILD SKILLS
## Phonics and Decoding

**LISTEN FOR *r*-CONTROLLED VOWELS /är/ *ar*, /ûr/ *ir, ur, er*** Blackline Master 42

**Alternate Teaching Strategy** Teacher's Edition p. T64

### Objectives
- To listen for *r*-controlled vowels /är/ *ar*, /ûr/ *ir, ur, er*
- To practice following directions
- To support hands-on learning

### Materials
One copy of Blackline Master 42 per child; crayons or colored pencils; scissors; pencils; paper

Invite children to color the first strip and top card one color. Have children color the second strip and bottom card another color. Show children how to cut along the dotted lines in each card and place the matching color strip through the resulting slits. Have children slide the strip to reveal one letter at a time. Encourage children to write the words they make on a sheet of paper. Have children read their new words.

**INFORMAL ASSESSMENT**

Display story pages 234–235 for children. Have children find words containing /är/ and /ûr/ sounds. One child can read page 234 while the other listens, and they can switch roles for page 235. Have pairs write their words on the chalkboard. For the /är/ sound, repeat the exercise with page 228.

## Phonics and Decoding

**CUMULATIVE REVIEW /är/, /ûr/, /ou/, /oi/, /ü/** Blackline Master 43

**Alternate Teaching Strategy** Teacher's Edition p. T72

### Objectives
- To reinforce phonemic awareness through review
- To practice following directions

### Materials
One copy of Blackline Master 43 per child; pencils

Go over the page with children. Explain that it contains words with some of the vowel sounds you have recently been studying. Discuss the pictures with children and prompt them to name each picture. Read aloud each word pair beside the picture. Have children choose and circle the correct word to match the picture. Tell them to write that word on the line provided.

**INFORMAL ASSESSMENT**

Page through the story text to find and read words containing the /är/, /ü/, /ûr/, /ou/, and /oi/ sounds. Make a list of words on the chalkboard for children to read aloud.

## Comprehension

**MAKING INFERENCES** Blackline Master 44

**Alternate Teaching Strategy** Teacher's Edition p. T69

### Objectives
- To review making inferences
- To follow directions

### Materials

One copy of Blackline Master 44 per child; pencils; crayons or colored pencils; scissors; glue or paste

Go over the page with children and read the title aloud. Then read aloud each speech balloon with children. Prompt children to name the characters in the pictures. Invite children to decide which character says the words in each speech bubble. Have children color and cut out each picture and glue it beside the corresponding speech bubble.

**INFORMAL ASSESSMENT**

To assess, direct children to the illustrations on pages 220–221. Ask children to tell you how the characters feel based only on the illustrations. (for instance, Jamaica seems hopeful; Ossie, annoyed) Then have children use story text or their own words to create speech bubbles for the pictures.

## Vocabulary Strategy

**COMPOUND WORDS**
Blackline Master 45

### Objectives
• To review compound words
• To practice following directions

**Alternate Teaching Strategy**
Teacher's Edition p. T71

### Materials

One copy of Blackline Master 45 per child; pencils

Remind children that a compound word is made by joining two smaller words. Explain that on this page children will make compound words by matching words from the cards (point to word cards) with those near the pictures (point to picture words) to describe the pictures. Then read aloud with children each word card and invite children to cut out the cards. Help children name each pictured object and sound out the word below the object. Tell children to choose the card that will create a compound word correctly naming the picture. Have children glue each card in place and then read aloud the resulting compound words.

**INFORMAL ASSESSMENT**

Assess children individually. Ask them to tell you the compound word for the game Jamaica wants to play with Ossie. (basketball) Have children find the word in story text or show you a basketball in story illustrations. Invite children to identify the smaller words that make up *basketball*. (basket and ball)

Name_____ Date_____

# Jamaica's Day

| Problem | Solution |
|---------|----------|
|         |          |

# Rhyming Word Cards

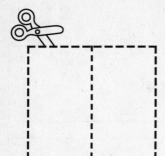

| c | f |
|---|---|
| p | s |
| ch | st |

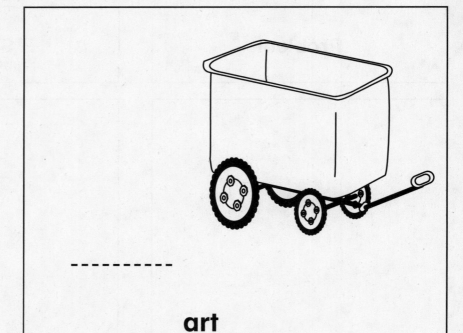

----------

**art**

----------

----------

**ir**

----------

Name _____ Date _____

# Name It

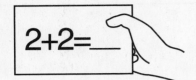

        card        cord

_____

_____

        house       hears

_____

_____

        stare       stew

_____

_____

        carp       curb

_____

_____

        toy       too

_____

_____

        bird       blue

_____

_____

# Who Said It?

"No. N-O, Jamaica. I told you not to tag along."

"It's not fair."

"Berto help!"

# You Can Make Compound Words

| spoon | ball | cutter | bow | boat | book |

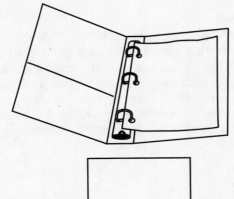

note

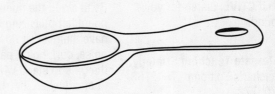

table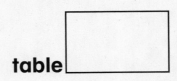

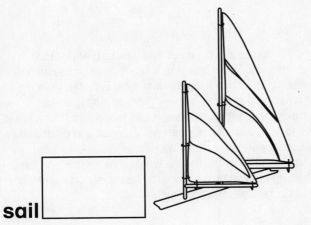

sail

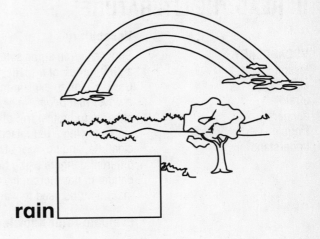

rain

snow

paper

# SHARKS pp. 244A–253R

## BUILD BACKGROUND FOR LANGUAGE SUPPORT

# I. FOCUS ON READING
## Focus on Skills

### Develop Phonological Awareness

**OBJECTIVE:** Listen for vowel sounds

Read aloud the poem, "Shark Food." Reread the words *boys* and *girls* from the poem, emphasizing the vowel sounds. Then separate the boys from the girls, and have them all sit down. Tell children that you will read a list of words. (whirl, toy, noise, curl, point, pearl, stir, join, twirl, shirt, coin, dirt, boil, soil, purr, void) Invite the girls to stand when they hear a word with the vowel sound in *girl* and the boys to stand when they hear a word with the vowel sound in *boy*. Repeat the process, pairing other words from "Shark Food" that have different vowel sounds.

**Alternate Teaching Strategy**
Teacher's Edition p. T64, T68, T70, T72

**TPR**

# II. READ THE LITERATURE

### Vocabulary

**VOCABULARY**
lesson
chew
afraid
danger
trouble
understand

Show children some safety signs, especially those without words. (For instance, a photograph of a "pedestrian crossing" sign that shows figures in a crosswalk.) Use the sign to explain the word *danger* by saying, for instance: *This sign tells a driver that people may be crossing a street. It warns drivers of a danger.* Ask children to brainstorm other existing symbolic warning signs (such as a "Don't Walk" sign showing a red raised hand, a "No Smoking" sign with a circled and crossed-out cigarette, and so on.) Challenge children to make a warning sign demonstrating different dangers using the vocabulary words. For the word *chew*, brainstorm the danger in not thoroughly chewing food and have students design symbols and signs that might be used to warn restaurant patrons accordingly.

### Evaluate Prior Knowledge

**CONCEPT**
sharks

**TPR**

Explain to children that sharks, like all living things, need food and a place to live. Show children pictures of sharks, including many different types. (hammerhead, great white, gray reef) Have children sort the pictures by type of shark. Then have children work in groups to develop comparisons and contrasts between sharks. Invite children to present their comments with words or pantomime. For example, children might show a picture of the largest shark and spread their arms wide to suggest size. A smaller shark could be shown with the symbol of finger and thumb an inch apart. As groups represent their comments, ask questions to generate additional comparisons and contrasts.

## Develop Oral Language

nonverbal prompt for active participation

- Preproduction: *Show us* (point to class and self) *your shark* (point to shark picture). *Show us how it is the same as* (point to a similar shark). *Show us how it is different from* (point to another shark).

one- or two-word response prompt

- Early production: *What is this?* (point to picture) *Can you tell me one way your shark is the same as the others? Can you tell me one way it is different?*

prompt for short answers to higher-level thinking skills

- Speech emergence: *What does this shark look like? Describe your shark and how it is the same or different from other sharks.*

prompt for detailed answers to higher-level thinking skills

- Intermediate fluency: *Why do you think people are afraid of sharks? What do you think is the scariest thing about your shark? What about the other sharks in these pictures? Which shark seems least scary? Why?*

# Guided Reading

### Preview and Predict

Tell children that they will read some true information about sharks in this article. They will learn from this story some ways sharks are in danger from people. Lead children on a picture walk, using the story's illustrations to reinforce concepts of sharks. Ask: *Can you point to a picture of a shark? Do you think this picture shows a shark? What do you think this shark is doing?* Point to the parts of a shark that might scare people. *Which shark do you think looks like a hammer? How do you think scientists protect themselves from sharks?*

**GRAPHIC ORGANIZER**
Blackline Master 46

### Objectives

- To reinforce making inferences
- To reinforce working together cooperatively
- To reinforce fact identification

### Materials

One copy of Blackline Master 46 per child; pencils; child copy of *Sharks*

Pair an English-speaking child with one needing language support. Model how to identify and record facts from the story in the left-hand column. (For example, *people kill 100 million sharks each year.*) Then discuss what this means about people's feelings toward sharks. Help children infer that people don't like sharks. Read the article with children. Invite partners to make other inferences about sharks as they read. Fluent children can record in words what their less fluent partners draw, pantomime, or explain with the selection photos. Encourage children to share their work with the class.

Reinforce the skill of making inferences. Have children read "Super Shark Facts" to a partner. Tell children to work together to make inferences about sharks from these facts.

# III. BUILD SKILLS
## Comprehension

**MAKE INFERENCES**
Blackline Master 47

**Alternate Teaching Strategy**
Teacher's Edition p. T69

### Objectives
• To reinforce making inferences
• To practice following direction

### Materials
One copy of Blackline Master 47 per child; crayons or colored pencils; scissors; glue or paste

Invite children to color and cut out the animals at the top of the page. Read aloud the title of the page. Tell children that each animal plays a role in one of the first two scenes shown on the page. Prompt children to describe what happened in each of the scenes and glue the animal in the appropriate scene. Ask children to complete the last scene by drawing what they think happened. Encourage children to share their drawings with each other.

**INFORMAL ASSESSMENT**

Direct children to page 248 of the article. Ask them how they think this picture was taken. Where was the photographer? (inside the cage).

## Comprehension

**MAKE INFERENCES**
Blackline Master 48

**Alternate Teaching Strategy**
Teacher's Edition p. T69

### Objectives
• To reinforce identifying problems and solutions
• To practice following directions

### Materials
One copy of Blackline Master 48 per child; crayons or colored pencils

Help children describe what is happening in the scene at the top of the page. Ask them: *What problems do these children have?* (It is raining on them.) Have children draw a picture in the box showing how the children could solve their problem.

**INFORMAL ASSESSMENT**

Have children return to the article text to identify one problem facing sharks (death by humans) and a possible solution (limits on shark killing).

# Vocabulary Strategy

**COMPOUND WORDS**
Blackline Master 49

**Alternate Teaching Strategy**
Teacher's Edition p. T71

**INFORMAL ASSESSMENT**

## Objectives
- To reinforce compound words
- To reinforce working cooperatively

## Materials

Two copies of Blackline Master 49 per child; crayons or colored pencils; glue or paste; tag board; scissors; paper

Help children color the first strip and card one color. Have children write the word *any* on the first rectangle in the first box, then write *some* on the second rectangle in that box. Next, have children color the second strip and card another color, writing the word *sun* on the first rectangle in the second box and *moon* on the remaining rectangle. Show children how to glue their cards and strips to pieces of tag board after cutting them them apart. Model the use of a word slide and have children follow you to make various compound words. Invite children to repeat each word with you as it is constructed.

Read aloud the caption text on page 247. Ask children to identify the compound word (hammerhead) and name its parts. (hammer, head)

# Vocabulary Strategy

**PREFIXES *re-, un-***
Blackline Master 50

**Alternate Teaching Strategy**
Teacher's Edition p. T67

**INFORMAL ASSESSMENT**

## Objectives
- To review prefixes *re-* and *un-*
- To practice following directions

## Materials

One copy of Blackline Master 50 per child; pencils

Remind children that *re-* means "again" and that *un-* means "not." Prompt children to describe what is happening in each picture. Then read the word under each picture and have children decide which prefix to add to correctly describe the picture. Ask children to write the complete word on the line below the picture.

Show children the picture on page 246. Ask: *Is someone who is not scared of this shark* unafraid *or* reafraid*?* (unafraid)

Name _____ Date _____

# Shark Facts

| Facts | Inferences |
|---|---|
| | |

Name _____ Date _____

# How Did It Happen?

# What Can They Do?

# Word Slides

| where | one | place | thing |
|---|---|---|---|
| beam | rise | light | shine |

## Word Beginnings

**any**                                    **some**

**sun**                                    **moon**

# Redo or Undo?

re-  un-

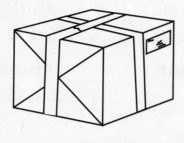

opened

_____

_____

re-  un-

afraid

_____

_____

re-  un-

play

_____

_____

re-  un-

place

_____

_____

re-  un-

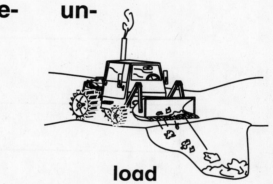

load

_____

_____

re-  un-

read

_____

_____

# ARTHUR WRITES A STORY pp. 258A–289R

Written and Illustrated by Marc Brown

## BUILD BACKGROUND FOR LANGUAGE SUPPORT

## I. FOCUS ON READING

### Focus on Skills

**OBJECTIVE:** Recognize silent letters

**Alternate Teaching Strategy**
Teacher's Edition p. T64

**TPR**
Use body language and physical response to demonstrate recognition of silent letters.

### Develop Phonological Awareness

Write the word *Bingo* on the chalkboard. Introduce the concept of silent letters by inviting children to sing the traditional song "Bingo." Point out that each time children clap, one or more of the letters are missing or silent. Then read the poem "Chalk Drawings" and write the word *chalk* on the board. Have children repeat after you, as you use the same tune to sing *"There was a teacher had a tool and chalk was its name-o . . . c-h-a-(clap)-k."* Make up new verses using other words from "Chalk Drawings" with silent letters.

## II. READ THE LITERATURE

### Vocabulary

**VOCABULARY**
important
decided
library
float
planet
proud

Print the vocabulary words on the chalkboard. Read each sentence and have the children guess the meaning of the underlined word. List each suggestion on the board then read each sentence with the suggested definition. Have children act out each sentence with the new definition. Have the class vote on which new defintion is closest to the unknown word. Have children turn to the page in their books as you read the sentence.

*Important:* p. 262 *"Write about something that is <u>important</u> to you."*

*Float:* p. 268 *"Scientifically speaking, elephants would weigh less on the moon, but wouldn't <u>float</u> that high," said the Brain*

*Library:* p. 271 *Arthur hurried to the <u>library</u>. "What are all those books for?" asked Francine.*

*Planet:* p. 273 *"Purple corn and blue elephants! On <u>Planet</u> Shmellafint!"*

*Decided:* p. 276 *He <u>decided</u> to turn his story into a song.*

*Proud:* p. 282 *Arthur told how <u>proud</u> he was of his pet business and how scared he was when Perky disappeared.*

### Evaluate Prior Knowledge

**CONCEPT**
pleasing others
be yourself

• Dramatize the concept of pleasing others by saying or doing things that will please them. For example, walk around the classroom and pick up a dropped pencil; compliment the color a child is wearing; admire the way a child is sitting up straight. Ask students what they think you are doing. Repeat examples until the children arrive at the answer. (you are doing and saying things to please others)

• Model for children something that you enjoy doing and that makes you feel good about yourself, such as participating in a sport. Say: *I like to swim. It makes me feel strong and healthy.* Ask: *What do you enjoy doing that makes you feel good about yourself?*

Invite children to pantomime or demonstrate something they enjoy doing and that pleases them. Children may wish to work individually, or in small groups to create situations such as those modeled by you.

### Develop Oral Language

nonverbal prompt for active participation

one- or two-word response prompt

prompt for short answers to higher-level thinking skills

prompt for detailed answers to higher-level thinking skills

- Preproduction: *Show us* (Point to class and self) *how you feel* (point to your face) *while you (do selected activity, make craft, play specific sport).*

- Early production: *Have you* (name activity) *for a long time? Is it something you like to do alone or with a friend?*

- Speech emergence: *What is your activity called? Where do you (play it, make it, choose correct label)? Was it easy or difficult to learn?*

- Intermediate fluency: *How do you feel when you do your favorite activity? Why do you enjoy it? Where did you learn how to do it?*

# Guided Reading

### Preview and Predict

Tell children that in this story Arthur is nervous about a homework assignment his teacher has given him. Explain that when Arthur is told to write a story, he decides to write about something he likes a lot, his puppy. Tell children: *Arthur shares his story with his sister and learns that she does not like it. Arthur starts to worry and wonder if he should write a story about what he really likes or should he try to write a story that will please others.* Then pair English-speaking children with those needing additional language support. Lead children on a picture walk using the story illustrations to reinforce the concepts of pleasing others and being yourself. Have one child answer the questions as the fluent speaker records answers on paper. Ask questions such as: *What is Arthur doing when he gets home from school? Who does he read his story to first? What do you think he is doing at the library? Who does he talk to about his story? When he reads to his family, do they seem to like his work? What do you think happens at the end?*

**GRAPHIC ORGANIZER**
Blackline Master 51

### Objectives

- To reinforce understanding of the main events and story details
- To support hands-on learning
- To reinforce working together cooperatively

### Materials

One copy of Blackline Master 51 per child; pencils, colored pencils, or crayons; student copy of *Arthur Writes a Story*

Go over the story map with children. Explain that the four boxes are for the four important things that happen in *Arthur Writes a Story*. Page through the story as a group and discuss possibilities for main ideas. Record possible keywords on the chalkboard with page numbers. As children who can read at grade level complete the chart with written text, children needing language support may draw the four main events. Encourage children who are able, to write a one- to two-word description of the event or a short sentence under the picture. Children can work individually or in pairs, where one child is completing the map with words and one with pictures.

Reinforce the skill of main events and story details. Have children use the illustrations on their story maps to retell *Arthur Writes a Story* to each other.

© McGraw-Hill School Division

# III. BUILD SKILLS

## Phonics and Decoding

**SILENT LETTERS**
Blackline Master 52

**Alternate Teaching Strategy**
Teacher's Edition p. T64

**Objectives**
- To recognize silent letters *b, k, w, g, l,* and *gh* in words
- To read words with silent letters *b, k, w, g, l,* and *gh*
- To practice working cooperatively

**Materials**
One copy of Blackline Master 52 per child; crayons or colored pencils

Go over the page with children. Explain that one of the pictures next to each word tells about the word. Give children these directions: *Read the word. Then tell what both pictures show. Decide which picture shows the word. Color the picture you choose.* Model the first row for them. Say the word *walk* and then say aloud what the two picture choices show: *a girl walking* and *a wall.* If necessary, read each word aloud slowly for them.

**INFORMAL ASSESSMENT**
To assess recognition of words with silent letters, have children work in pairs. Direct them to the story text, for example to page 268. Tell them to identify a word on the page with a silent letter or letters. (weigh) Call on teams to share the word and to tell which letter(s) is silent.

## Phonics and Decoding

**REVIEW SILENT LETTERS**
Blackline Master 53

**Alternate Teaching Strategy**
Teacher's Edition p. T64

**Objectives**
- To recognize silent letters: *k, b, l, w, g, gh*
- To read silent letter words
- To practice following directions

**Materials**
One copy of Blackline Master 53 per child; one sheet of construction paper per child; scissors; paste or glue; crayons or colored pencils (optional)

Explain to children that the pictures and the words on the page are mixed up. Tell them that each word has a picture that matches what it says. Provide the following directions: *Cut out the squares. Find the squares that have the words in them. Glue the word squares on the paper down the side in one column. Read the words. Then look at the picture squares. Find the picture square that shows what each word square says. Glue the picture square that matches next to the word square on the construction paper.* Children may color if desired.

**INFORMAL ASSESSMENT**
Direct children to page 274. Select two words from the page, one containing a silent letter and one that does not, such as *talking* and *last.* Write them on the chalkboard and say the words aloud. Ask children to identify the word with the silent letter. Repeat using words from other pages, such as *weigh, that; high, on* from page 268.

# Comprehension

**FANTASY AND REALITY**
Blackline Master 54

**Alternate Teaching Strategy**
Teacher's Edition p. T66

## Objectives
• To distinguish between fantasy and reality
• To practice following directions

Materials

One copy of Blackline Master 54 per child; scissors; colored pencils or crayons; paste or glue

Go over the page with the children. Read the chart headings *Real* and *Make-Believe* to them. Discuss each picture briefly. Then divide children into pairs or small groups. Invite children to color all the pictures and glue or paste the picture under the correct category heading. Invite children to explain why they placed each picture in its place.

**INFORMAL ASSESSMENT**

Tell children to look at the illustrations on pages 266 and 267. Ask children to share something real and make-believe from the illustrations. (real: one person is reading to another; make-believe: the elephant is floating above the moon) Allow them to share additional examples from other pages.

# Vocabulary Strategy

**REVIEW CONTEXT CLUES**
Blackline Master 55

**Alternate Teaching Strategy**
Teacher's Edition p. T67

## Objectives
• To use word order and other context clues to figure out the meaning of unfamiliar words
• To practice following directions

## Materials

One copy of Blackline Master 55 per child; pencils; crayons or colored pencils

For each item, read and discuss the sentences with children and the three word choices below. Point out the underlined word in each one. Tell children that one way to figure out the meaning of an unfamiliar word is to use clues from the other words in the sentence and from the picture. Tell children to read each word choice again, and circle the word or words that have nearly the same meaning as the underlined word. Encourage children to check their answer choice by reading the sentence aloud and substituting the word or words they circled for the underlined word. This activity may work best if children are paired with more fluent readers or as a teacher-directed activity. Children may color the pictures if desired.

**INFORMAL ASSESSMENT**

Have children locate and then use their hands to isolate the word *research* on page 271. Say: *Let's read the sentences and look at the picture to figure out what this word means.* Repeat, having child pairs take turns choosing words and sharing meanings with each other.

# Sequence of Events

```
┌─────────────────────────────────────────────┐
│                                               │
│                                               │
│                                               │
│                                               │
└─────────────────────────────────────────────┘
                      ↓

┌─────────────────────────────────────────────┐
│                                               │
│                                               │
│                                               │
│                                               │
└─────────────────────────────────────────────┘
                      ↓

┌─────────────────────────────────────────────┐
│                                               │
│                                               │
│                                               │
│                                               │
└─────────────────────────────────────────────┘
                      ↓

┌─────────────────────────────────────────────┐
│                                               │
│                                               │
│                                               │
│                                               │
└─────────────────────────────────────────────┘
```

# Silent Letters

**walk**

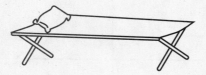

**knot**

**write**

**light**

**comb**

**sign**

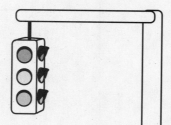

# Picture-Word Match

| knee | thumb | calf |
| --- | --- | --- |

| wrote | night | sign |
| --- | --- | --- |

# Real or Make-Believe?

**Real** **Make-Believe**

# What Kind of Word Is It?

**1.** The bell rings. Sam <u>hurries</u> to the door.

     **boy**       **runs**       **fast**

**2.** The little elephant was just a baby.
The <u>gigantic</u> elephant was its mother.

     **big**       **animal**       **cared**

**3.** Did he <u>create</u> the story without help?

     **reader**       **make up**       **alone**

**4.** <u>Several</u> children liked the story.

     **many**       **clapped**       **loudly**

**5.** Can't you find your shoes? Did you
look <u>beneath</u> the bed?

     **hunt**       **lost**       **under**

# BEST WISHES, ED pp. 290A–319R

Written and Illustrated by James Stevenson

## BUILD BACKGROUND FOR LANGUAGE SUPPORT

## I. FOCUS ON READING

### Focus on Skills

**OBJECTIVE:** listen for /ər/er

**Alternate Teaching Strategy**
Teacher's Edition p. T68

**TPR**

#### Develop Phonological Awareness

Write the word *teacher* on the chalkboard. Ask children what sound they hear at the end of the word. Point to yourself to provide context for the word. Then say and emphasize words that contain this sound from the poem, "The Visit". (mother, brother, sister)

Display two jars, one labeled *er* and one without a label. Show children cards printed with /ər/ words, as well as cards displaying words that do not contain the sound. Chose a word card, say the word *teacher*, and ask children in which jar the word belongs. Have volunteers put cards into the appropriate jars, pointing to themselves when a word such as sister applies to them. Reproduce "The Visit" and distribute to children (or transfer it to an overhead transparency), and invite children to circle or identify words with /ər/.

## II. READ THE LITERATURE

**VOCABULARY**
climbed
couple
drifted
half
message
notice

**TPR**

**CONCEPT**
special abilities

#### Vocabulary

Print the vocabulary words on the board and on individual cards. Read together and discuss each word. Using chalkboard sketches and classroom objects, such as a toy boat drifting in a bowl of water, help children to picture as many words as possible. Write sentences on the board containing the remaining words. Ask one child to point to an object, sketch, or written word, as another child says that word.

Play a game of "Picture This!" Divide children into two teams. Privately, so that other players do not see, show a member of each team the same word card. These two children then draw a depiction of the vocabulary word on the chalkboard while their teammates attempt to guess which one it is.

#### Evaluate Prior Knowledge

Tell children about a special ability you have, such as drawing or playing a musical instrument. Model your special ability for children if possible. Reinforce the concept of special abilities by asking students to list the unique skills of specific sports, entertainment, and other cultural figures, as well as those of characters in familiar stories. (For example, Michael Jordan's special ability is playing basketball.) Ask: *What are some of your special abilities?* Invite children to pantomime or demonstrate those special abilities. You may also want to plan a day when students (and, perhaps, their parents) can demonstrate their special talents, skills, and abilities.

## Develop Oral Language

nonverbal prompt for active participation

- Preproduction: *Show us* (point to class and self) y*our special ability.* (Repeat your modeling of your special ability. Then help children name and describe their special ability.) *You are a* (dancer, skater, painter)*, I see.*

one- or two-word response prompt

- Early production: *What is your ability called? How long have you* (name ability)*? Do you take lessons?*

prompt for short answers to higher-level thinking skills

- Speech emergence: *Was your special ability easy or difficult to learn? When do you practice? What do you like best about your ability?*

prompt for detailed answers to higher-level thinking skills

- Intermediate fluency: *Can you tell us how you got interested in* (name ability)*? Did you have to study and try very hard to learn how to do it? Is there any other special ability you would like to learn how to do?*

## Guided Reading

### Preview and Predict

Tell children that in this story, Ed is a penguin who learns two important things: that everyone has special abilities and that things aren't always what they seem. Say: *Ed gets separated from his home, friends, and family. Then he discovers he has a special ability that helps him.* Use the story illustrations (pp. 297–297 and 298–299) to establish the concept of separation and to offer clues to Ed's special ability. As you lead children on a picture walk, prompt oral or kinesthetic responses to these questions: *Where do Ed and the penguins live? What is the climate? What happened to Ed's piece of ice? In what special way is Ed using his wing? What do you think Ed's special ability will turn out to be? What problem do you think Ed has? How do you think he might use that ability to solve his problem?*

**GRAPHIC ORGANIZER**
Blackline Master 56

### Objectives

- To reinforce distinction of realistic story events from those that are make-believe
- To support hands-on learning
- To reinforce working cooperatively

### Materials

One copy of Blackline Master 56 per child; pencils, colored pencils, or crayons; student copy of *Best Wishes, Ed*

Show the What's Real? chart to children. Explain, and model with examples, the concepts of fantasy and reality. Page through *Best Wishes, Ed* as a class, identifying the events that could really happen and those that are make-believe. Give children child notes or paper clips to mark these pictures in their books. Then have children complete the chart, either with drawings or with descriptions matching their fluency levels. Children will want to share their charts, as well as strategies for determining reality versus make-believe.

# III. BUILD SKILLS
## Phonics and Decoding

**REVIEW /ər/er**
Blackline Master 57

**Alternate Teaching Strategy**
Teacher's Edition p. T68

### Objectives
- To practice using and identifying /ər/er words
- To form /ər/er words from known base words
- To practice working cooperatively

### Materials
One copy of Blackline Master 57 per child; pencil; scissors; tag board

Ask children to cut apart the two word slips on the page. Read each word together. Help children create a word slide by cutting slits in the *er* card and threading a word slip through the slits. Model how to use the word strip to make a new word with *er*. Children can then use their word slides to create new words. Read the newly created words together. In pairs, one child can use the word slide to form a new word that the other student will act out.

**INFORMAL ASSESSMENT**

To assess children's ability to use words with the /ər/er sound, have them look at the illustration on page 304. Ask them to use the word *writer* in oral descriptions of Ed's actions on this page. Repeat the exercise using the word *wetter* and the story illustration on page 300.

## Phonics and Decoding

**REVIEW /ər/er AND SILENT LETTER**
Blackline Master 58

**Alternate Teaching Strategy**
Teacher's Edition p. T68

### Objectives
- To review /ər/er
- To review and practice reading silent letters: *l, b, w, g, gh*
- To practice following directions

### Materials
One copy of Blackline Master 58 per child; pencils; colored pencils or crayons

Explain to children that each picture on the page has part of a word written under it. Model how to add the letters *er* to each word part to create a word that tells about the picture. Ask children to read aloud the completed word, then invite them to identify the silent letter or letters in each word.

**INFORMAL ASSESSMENT**

Direct children back to page 312 of the story text. Tell children to find a word on the page that ends in *er*. (other) Ask them to say it aloud and try using it in a sentence.

# Comprehension

**INTRODUCE CAUSE AND EFFECT**
Blackline Master 59

**Alternate Teaching Strategy**
Teacher's Edition p. T69

**INFORMAL ASSESSMENT**

### Objectives
• To reinforce understanding of cause and effect relationships
• To practice following directions

### Materials
One copy of Blackline Master 59 per child; scissors; string or yarn; popsicle sticks or one hanger per child; colored pencils or crayons

Explain to children that each picture on their sheets shows something about to happen. Have children draw and, if possible, write to describe the effect of this event, or what has happened next. When children are done, have them complete the third pair with a cause and effect of their own. Help children construct their mobiles by first cutting apart each box, and gluing pictures of causes to the back of matching effects. Then help children punch holes in each card, thread them with string, and tie to coat hangers.

Direct children back to pages 298–299 of the text. Ask them to describe how Ed ended up on his own little patch of ice. Children can explain how this happened by either using short answers or by pointing to the appropriate details in this and other story illustrations.

# Vocabulary Strategy

**REVIEW CONTEXT CLUES**
Blackline Master 60

**Alternate Teaching Strategy**
Teacher's Edition p. T67

**INFORMAL ASSESSMENT**

### Objectives
• To use context clues, including word order, to understand meaning of unfamiliar words
• To practice following directions

### Materials
One copy of Blackline Master 60 per child; pencil; colored pencils or crayons (optional)

Have children read, or listen as you read, each of the dialogue bubbles on the page. Discuss what the pictures show and how the underlined word is used in the sentence. Ask children to tell which word in each box means the same thing as the underlined word in each dialogue bubble. Reread the sentences and word choices in each box, asking children to look closely at all clues to determine the answer. Let children color the pictures if they wish.

Have children refer to page 296 of the text and point to the word *cracking*. Say: *Let's read the sentences and look at the picture to figure out what this word could mean.* Call on several children for ideas, then discuss responses as a class to find the best one. Invite pairs of children to find unknown words in the text to define in a similar way. Come together as a whole class once again to discuss each pair's findings.

Name _____ Date _____

# What's Real?

| Fantasy | Reality |
|---------|---------|
|         |         |

# Word Slide

| | |
|---|---|
| camp | sing |
| fish | talk |
| mark | teach |
| paint | wait |

-------------

er

-------------

# Who or What?

answ_____

climb_____

firefight_____

knock_____

walk_____

writ_____

Grade 2

Name _____ Date _____

# Cause and Effect Mobile

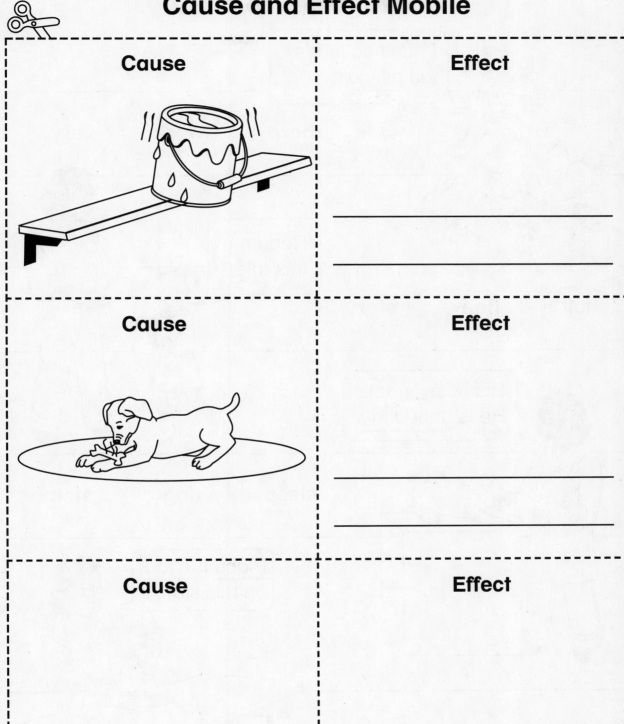

| Cause | Effect |
|---|---|
| | _____ |
| | _____ |
| Cause | Effect |
| | _____ |
| | _____ |
| Cause | Effect |
| | _____ |
| | _____ |

# What's the Word?

I can't do it. It's too <u>difficult</u>.

**hard**     **work**     **very**

Read me this <u>tale</u>.

**tell**     **fine**     **story**

His nose is hot. He is <u>unhealthy</u>.

**sleep**     **dog**     **sick**

<u>Place</u> the fork on this side.

**set**     **dish**     **next**

# THE PONY EXPRESS pp. 320A–341R

Written by Dale Ryder  Illustrated by Kunio Hagio

## BUILD BACKGROUND FOR LANGUAGE SUPPORT

## I. FOCUS ON READING
### Focus on Skills

**OBJECTIVE:** Listen for short *e*

**TPR**

### Develop Phonological Awareness

Read aloud the poem "Pony Express." Tell children to listen for the sound they hear in the middle of the word *head.* Say this word slowly so children can hear the vowel sound. Then direct children to place their hands on their head each time they hear a word with the noted sound. Play "Draw It," in which children listen as you call out pairs of words. Tell them one of the words has the same middle sound they hear in *head.* Have children draw the picture of the word with the short *e* sound. Word pair examples are: *hen, hand; pen, pond; log, leg; boat, bed.*

## II. READ THE LITERATURE

### Vocabulary

**VOCABULARY**
rushed
arrive
early
finished
record
success

Print the vocabulary words on the chalkboard. Read the following sentences aloud. Ask children to guess the meaning of each vocabulary word based on clues found in the sentences. If children can't determine meaning based on context clues, pantomime words where possible. Write their suggestions on the chalkboard, then read each sentence with the suggested definitions. Decide, as a class, the correct definitions.

*The mail will <u>arrive</u> in San Francisco in ten days.*

*The rider and horse are very fast. They <u>rushed</u> away as the crowd cheered.*

*The Pony Express riders were even faster today. They delivered the mail <u>early</u>.*

*When the rider arrived at the end of his route, he was <u>finished</u>.*

*Pony Express rider Buffalo Bill holds the <u>record</u> for the longest ride. He rode 384 miles in one trip.*

*The riders did such a good job, everyone said the Pony Express was a <u>success</u>.*

**CONCEPT**
types of communication

### Evaluate Prior Knowledge

Explain to children that there are many different ways of getting messages to people. Help children brainstorm some of these and list them on the chalkboard: *talking in person, telephone, writing notes or letters, body language, computer.* Model these methods as necessary to ensure understanding. Choose a simple message familiar to most children, such as: *Time to eat.* Organize children in cooperative groups of three or four. Assign each group of children a method of communication. Encourage them to pantomime or role-play in order to convey the assigned message. Invite other children to guess which mode of communication is being displayed.

## Develop Oral Language

While children are acting out their message, ask questions such as the following:

nonverbal prompt for active participation

- Preproduction: *Show us* (Point to class and self) *the message you want to send. Show us how you would send this message to someone who lived far away.* (Model writing a note or letter and making a phone call.)

one- or two-word response prompt

- Early production: *Tell me which way of communicating you like best? Point to the brainstormed choices on the chalkboard. Which way of communicating would your friend use to invite you over to play?*

prompt for short answers to higher-level thinking skills

- Speech emergence: *Have you ever sent someone a letter in the mail? Where do you put a letter when you want to send it? Is sending a letter the fastest way to tell someone a message?*

prompt for detailed answers to higher-level thinking skills

- Intermediate fluency: *Which do you think is the fastest way of telling someone a message? Which way do you think would take the longest? Why?*

# Guided Reading

## Preview and Predict

Tell children that this true story tells how mail used to be delivered by riders on horseback. Explain that the horses and riders had a very hard job to do. Lead children on a picture walk using the story illustrations to support the concept of types of communication. Ask questions such as: *What is the man in this picture doing? When and where do you think this story takes place? Where do you think the mail is put during the ride? What might the signs or arrows mean? What might make the jobs of the Pony Express riders and horses so hard? What kind of men do you think the riders shown here are?*

## Objectives

**GRAPHIC ORGANIZER**
Blackline Master 61

- To identify cause and effect relationships between events
- To practice following directions
- To reinforce story comprehension

**Alternate Teaching Strategy**
Teacher's Edition p. T69

## Materials

One copy of Blackline Master 61 per child; pencils; child copy of *The Pony Express*

Go over the chart with children. Explain that sometimes events in a story cause or make something else happen. Model how to list a cause in the left-hand box and an effect in the right-hand box. Discuss possibilities for the first box, such as *Johnnie wants a job; Johnnie rides for the Pony Express.* Pair children and allow fluent children to record responses in written language while those needing language support use illustrations.

Reinforce the skill of cause and effect. Have children ask and answer questions beginning *Why did _____ happen?*

# III. BUILD SKILLS

## Phonics and Decoding

**SHORT *e: ea***
Blackline Master 62

**Alternate Teaching Strategy**
Teacher's Edition p. T70

### Objectives
- To reinforce sound/symbol correspondence
- To practice following directions
- To identify words with short *e:ea*
- To read words with short *e:ea*

### Materials
One copy of Blackline Master 62 per child; scissors; colored pencils or crayons

Explain to children that the beginning sound for each pictured word is missing from the -*ead* letters in the middle of the page. Say: *Let's say the pictured words together and listen for the beginning letter that is missing.* Help children cut out the letter strip and word slide in the picture box. Demonstrate how to form words by inserting the strip. Choose a picture word and say it aloud. Ask children to manipulate their word slide to display the target word.

**INFORMAL ASSESSMENT**

Direct children back to story page 325 to find what the knapsack or *mochila* was made of. (leather) Print the answer on the board and ask a volunteer to identify which letters make the short *e* sound. *(ea)*

## Phonics and Decoding

**SILENT LETTERS**
Blackline Master 63

**Alternate Teaching Strategy**
Teacher's Edition p. T64, T68

### Objectives
- To reinforce recognition of spelling patterns
- To support hands-on learning
- To develop phonemic awareness

### Materials
One copy of Blackline Master 63 per child; colored pencils or crayons; scissors; glue or paste; construction paper or oaktag

Ask children to say aloud what each picture shows. Have them color the pictures and then cut out both picture and word squares along the dotted lines. Show children how to make flashcards by pasting the picture and matching word square to opposite sides of a piece of oaktag. Children can work in pairs to play matching games.

**INFORMAL ASSESSMENT**

Direct children back to the story text. Ask children to name the English word for the container in which letters were carried. (knapsack) Ask them which letter in this word is silent, and ask them to find the word using their picture/word card activity.

## Comprehension

**FANTASY AND REALITY**
Blackline Master 64

**Alternate Teaching Strategy**
Teacher's Edition p. T66

### Objectives
- To reinforce the difference between real and make-believe
- To encourage creative thinking in generating explanations
- To practice following directions

### Materials

One copy of Blackline Master 64 per child; colored pencils or crayons in two colors; scissors

Tell children to color the pictures, using one color for pictures they think are real and a second color for pictures they think are make-believe. Have children cut out the pictures on the dotted lines. Say: *Put the "real" pictures on one side of your desk and the "make-believe" pictures on the other side of your desk.* Encourage children to make observations about the difference between the two groups. Ask them to name each group as *real* or *make-believe.*

**INFORMAL ASSESSMENT**

Tell children to look at the illustrations in the story *The Pony Express.* Ask children whether they think the pictures show something real. Ask them to explain their responses. (Yes, the people look like they could really exist and the actions look like they could really happen.)

## Vocabulary Strategy

**SYNONYMS**
Blackline Master 65

**Alternate Teaching Strategy**
Teacher's Edition p. T71

### Objectives

• To recognize words with similar meaning
• To practice following directions

### Materials

One copy of Blackline Master 65 per pair of children; scissors

Have children cut out the squares from the top part of the page along the dotted lines. Then say a word from the bottom grid, such as *mail.* Tell children that one of the words they cut out means nearly the same thing as *mail.* Model finding the synonym for *mail,* saying: *Look for the word card that says "letters." When you find it, place it over the word on your chart that says "mail."*

**INFORMAL ASSESSMENT**

Refer children back to the text and ask them to identify a word from the chart, such as *letters.* Ask a volunteer to read the sentence aloud, and substitute the synonym partner from the chart for that word in the sentence. Repeat using different synonym word pairs.

# Cause and Effect

**Effect**

**Cause**

# Word Slide

ah

br

h

l

r

spr

thr

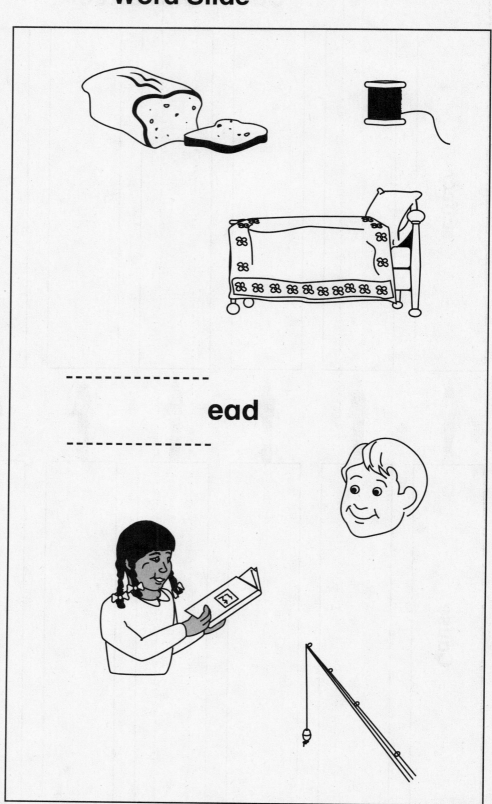

ead

# Picture-Word Cards

| | | |
|---|---|---|
| **knapsack** | **doughnut** | **feather** |
|  | 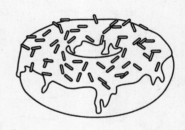 (feather image) | (doughnut image) |
| **half** | **signed** | **climb** |
| 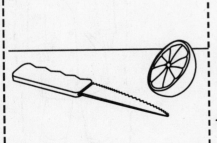 |  |  |

# Real or Make-Believe

# Tic-Tac-Word

| | | |
|---|---|---|
| carry | change | cheer |
| fast | letters | rushed |
| see | ship | start |

| | | |
|---|---|---|
| mail | watch | take |
| shout | dashed | boat |
| quick | trade | begin |

# NINE-IN ONE, GRR! GRR! pp. 342A–369R

### Adapted by Cathy Spagnoli  Illustrated by Nancy Hom

## BUILD BACKGROUND FOR LANGUAGE SUPPORT

## I. FOCUS ON READING
### Focus on Skills

**OBJECTIVE:** Listen for long *e*

**Alternate Teaching Strategy**
Teacher's Edition p. T72

**TPR**
Utilize and develop visual aides to demonstrate recognition of long *e*.

### Develop Phonological Awareness

Display an index card with a key shown on it and make the long *e* sound for children. Hold it up and say: *We hear the /ē/ sound when we say* key. Distribute five index cards to each child. Read the poem "Tiger's Friends", asking children to hold up an index card each time they hear /ē/. Pause to repeat the long /e/ word from the poem, then help children write the word on an index card. Where appropriate, have children illustrate their cards. Then reread the poem, giving children an opportunity to raise the corresponding card when they hear the word.

## II. READ THE LITERATURE

**VOCABULARY**
Earth
lonely
wonderful
forget
mountain
memory

**CONCEPT**
animals in folk tale

### Vocabulary

Print the vocabulary words on the board. Provide a brief demonstration of each of the words using the following suggestions. Pause after each demonstration and point to the word on the board. Pronounce it, use it in context, then ask children to pronounce it and mimic your demonstration.

*Earth:* Point to a picture of the Earth in space, and show a globe. Say: *We live on this planet called Earth.*

*lonely:* Stand far away from the rest of the class and say: *I am lonely. Please join me.* Invite each child to join you, one at a time, until only one child is left. Say, for example, *Kristina looks lonely. Let's join her.*

*wonderful:* Provide slices of apples or bananas to each child. Taste a slice and say: *This is wonderful!* Have a flower nearby, smell it and ask: *How does this smell?* Prompt children to respond: *The flower smells wonderful.*

*forget and memory:* Draw five simple pictures or shapes on the chalkboard. Allow a brief moment for children to look at them. Then erase the board and say: *Use your memory and tell me what you saw on the board.* If children can't remember them all, ask: *Did you forget?*

*mountain:* Show pictures of mountains from books or magazines. If possible, show pictures of mountain climbers. Say: *Let's climb a mountain.* Pantomime climbing a mountain and ask children to join you.

### Evaluate Prior Knowledge

Explain that in some stories, animals act and talk like people. Show children a non-fiction animal story with photographs or realistic illustrations of animals. Then show them a folk tale with stylistic illustrations of talking animals. Ask (pointing to the realistic story): *What do these animals say?* (various animal noises) Ask (pointing to the folk tale): *What do these animals say?* (for instance, *Hello. How are you?*)

Tell children that the story they are about to read is a folk tale from the country of Laos, in Southeast Asia. Explain that a folk tale is a story about people or animals that grown-ups first told their children long, long ago. When those children became grown-ups they told their children, and so on. In a folk tale, animals may talk and act like humans. Invite children to share traditional stories from their own cultures. Provide picture books of folk tales that represent the cultures of children in the classroom.

## Develop Oral Language

nonverbal prompt for active participation

• Preproduction: *Show us* (point to class and self) *something that a real animal does.*

one- or two-word response prompt

• Early production: *Can you tell us one thing that a real animal does? Can you tell us one thing an animal from a folk tale might do?*

prompt for short answers to higher-level thinking skills

• Speech emergence: *Can you tell us something that a real animal would not do that the animals in stories do? Why wouldn't a real animal do that?*

prompt for detailed answers to higher-level thinking skills

• Intermediate fluency: *What is your favorite animal character and from which folk tale does it come? Why is it your favorite? Is it a funny or scary character?*

# Guided Reading

## Preview and Predict

Tell children that in this story the main characters are animals who do some things as humans would. One animal, Tiger, makes up a little song to help her remember some important information. Another character, Bird, wants Tiger to forget the information.

Lead children on a picture walk through the story. Use illustrations to reinforce the concept of imaginary folk tale by explaining that, in the illustration on page 349, Tiger is asking a man a question.  Ask children to help you find other pictures in the tale where an animal appears to be speaking. (p. 359, 361) Possible questions to pose in relation to these illustrations are: *What do you think Tiger is asking the man? Why is Tiger thinking of all those little tigers? What do you think the man tells the tiger? What do you think Bird is asking the man?  What might happen at the end of the story?* Help less fluent children to respond with body language or drawings.

## Objectives

• To reinforce understanding of reality and fantasy
• To reinforce working together cooperatively

**GRAPHIC ORGANIZER**
Blackline Master 66

## Materials

One copy of Blackline Master 66 per child; pencils; child copy of *Nine-in-One, Grr! Grr!*

Go over the Reality and Fantasy chart with children. Review that animals in this story do things that real animals cannot and would not do. As you read the story, tell children to think about which of Tiger's and Bird's actions could be real and which could not. Direct children to record the actions on their charts, using the story illustrations for help. Tell them to list the way real animals would act on the *reality* side and the way animals do in the story on the *fantasy* side. Children can record their thoughts in written language or with pictures and one- or two-word responses as appropriate to their fluency. Urge children to explain their completed charts to one another, using body language such as nodding the head to show "yes" or "no" that an action is realistic.

© McGraw-Hill School Division

# III. BUILD SKILLS
## Phonics and Decoding

**LONG *e: y, ey***
Blackline Master 67

**Alternate Teaching Strategy**
Teacher's Edition p. T72

### Objectives
• To recognize the long *e* sound
• To distinguish between *y* and *ey*
• To practice following directions

### Materials
One copy of Blackline Master 67 per child; crayons or colored pencils of two different colors; scissors

Tell children to use one color to shade the box next to the letter *y*, and another color to shade the box next to the letters *ey*. List the word parts from the first column of the chart on the chalkboard (*cit-, happ-, man-, funn-*). Invite children to shade these boxes the same color they chose for *y*. On the chalkboard, list the word parts from the remaining four boxes in the second column (*donk-, hon-, monk-, turk-*). Ask students to cut apart these squares, shade them the same color they used for the *ey* box, then match them accordingly. Together, read each new word.

**INFORMAL ASSESSMENT**

To assess recognition of the long *e* sound, allow children to work in pairs to skim the story, looking for words that have the long *e* sound and end in *y* or *ey* with that sound. Have them write the beginning letters on the empty square from the word maker, and place it in the *y* word box to create a new word. Have children say the new word.

## Phonics and Decoding

**CUMULATIVE REVIEW**
Blackline Master 68

**Alternate Teaching Strategy**
Teacher's Edition p. T72

### Objectives
• To review and reinforce use of context skills and letter sound correspondence to read unfamiliar words
• To practice following directions

### Materials
One copy of Blackline Master 68 per child; colored pencils or crayons

Explain that each box on the page gives a drawing direction. Tell children to use clues from the words and the sounds the letters make to decide what to draw. Review some of the silent letters on the page (such as *gh* in *night*), then read the sentences with children, encouraging them to decode as many words as possible. Have children draw appropriate drawings and share these with each other.

**INFORMAL ASSESSMENT**

To assess children's knowledge of silent letters, the /ə r/*er* sound and long *e* sound, ask children to turn to page 352 and find one word that demonstrates each of these phonics skills. (*memory, thought, Tiger*)

# Comprehension

**REVIEW CAUSE AND EFFECT**
Blackline Master 69

**Alternate Teaching Strategy**
Teacher's Edition p. T69

### Objectives
• To recognize cause and effect relationships
• To work cooperatively
• To encourage creative thinking

### Materials
One copy of Blackline Master 69 per child; pencil; colored pencils or crayons

Discuss the picture in the first box with children. Explain that the event pictured is going to cause or make something happen. Discuss possible effects, or results. Have children draw and/or write the effect. Repeat this process with the second box. In the third box, have children develop their own cause and effect picture sequence and add one- or two-word captions. If children have difficulty brainstorming ideas for their cause-and-effect boxes, encourage them to use events from the story. Invite children to share their cause-and-effect boxes with each other.

**INFORMAL ASSESSMENT**

Direct children back to the text. Ask them to search the story and pictures for other cause-and-effect examples, such as when Bird flaps her wings and then Tiger looks up. Discuss children's ideas as a class.

# Vocabulary Strategy

**REVIEW SYNONYMS**
Blackline Master 70

**Alternate Teaching Strategy**
Teacher's Edition p. T71

### Objectives
• To reinforce recognition of words with similar meaning
• To practice word identification

### Materials
One copy of Blackline Master 70 per child; scissors; crayons or colored pencil of two different colors; construction paper or oak tag; glue or paste

Ask children to shade the boxes on the top half of the page using one color, and the boxes on the bottom half using another color. Explain that sometimes different words have almost the same meanings. Read the word boxes slowly. Then have children cut out the words. Tell them to paste onto construction paper word pairs with similar meanings. For children needing extra support, say one words as they search to find its synonym.

**INFORMAL ASSESSMENT**

Read aloud the first sentence of the story on page 374 to children. Then say: *Find and look at the word* many. *I want you to think of a synonym, or word that means almost the same thing, and read the sentence out loud using the new word.* Repeat with other appropriate words and sentences.

Name _____ Date _____

# Reality/Fantasy Chart

| Reality | Fantasy |
|---------|---------|
|         |         |

# Word Maker

| | |
|---|---|
| cit | donk |
| happ | hon |
| man | |
| tin | monk |
| mon | turk |

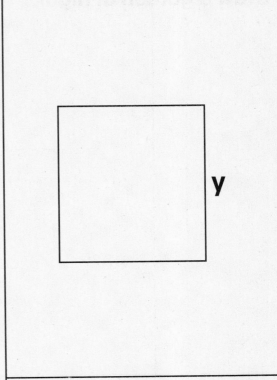

y

ey

# Read and Draw

| **Draw a garden at night.** | **Draw half a doughnut.** |
|---|---|
| **Draw eleven feathers.** | **Draw a climbing monkey.** |

Name _____ Date _____

# What Happened?

**Cause**         **Effect**

_____

_____

**Cause**        **Effect**

_____

_____

**Cause**        **Effect**

_____

_____

Name _____ Date _____

# Find the Match

| | |
|---|---|
| small | speak |
| glad | every |
| nearer | listen |
| cubs | path |
| open | stop |

| | |
|---|---|
| end | happy |
| each | talk |
| babies | hear |
| unlock | tiny |
| closer | road |

# CHANGE FOR THE QUARTER pp. 370A–379R

## BUILD BACKGROUND FOR LANGUAGE SUPPORT

## I. FOCUS ON READING

### Focus on Skills

**OBJECTIVE:** Review silent letters, long *e*, short *e*, and /ə/ sounds

**Alternate Teaching Strategy**
Teacher's Edition p. T64, T68, T70, T72

**TPR**

### Develop Phonological Awareness

Read aloud the poem "Fifty Cents." Explain that you are going to play a game where children have to match words to sounds. Write the following on the board: *shorter, tickle, Fred, bee*. Say each word aloud, stressing the vowel sounds. Then reread the poem, word by word. Pause repeatedly to say a poem word and then say each of the words on the board. Have the class give thumbs up if they think the poem word has the same sound as one of the words on the board. Invite volunteers to write each poem word discussed under the posted heading on the chalkboard.

## II. READ THE LITERATURE

### Vocabulary

**VOCABULARY**
join
collect
honors
order
pocket
worth

Print the vocabulary words on the board. Say the words and have children pronounce them after you. Have children copy the words onto index cards. Then take children on a walk around school and demonstrate the vocabulary words in the following way:

*join:* Walk to the principal's office, or to another available adult in the school and say: *We're going on a walk. Would you like to join us?* Ask children to hold up the index card for the word *join*.

*collect:* Walk to the library and find books about stamp collections (or baseball cards, coins, etc.) Say: *Some people collect stamps. Do you collect anything?* If possible, ask the librarian if he or she collects anything. Have children show the index card for the word *collect*.

*honors:* Before you leave the room, prepare a simple certificate that reads *Good Lunches Award*. Walk to the lunchroom and present award to the manager and say: *Our class honors you with this award.* Have children show the card for the word *honors*.

*order:* Walk outside with children and say: *Let's line up in order of our height. I am the tallest, I'll stand at the back of the line. Where will you stand?* You may want to arrange the children, or you may have someone help with this. Once lined up, ask children to hold up their cards showing the word *order*.

*pocket:* Reach into your pocket and pull out a quarter, a nickel, a dime, and a penny. Say: *Look what I found in my pocket!* Ask children to find the card for the word *pocket*.

*worth:* Show the coins and ask if anyone knows how much each is worth. Prompt them by saying: *This penny is worth one cent.*

**CONCEPT**
the changing quarter

## Evaluate Prior Knowledge

Invite children to tell about coins they know from other countries. Then show a quarter to children and tell them its value. Allow children to pass it around, encouraging them to feel the front and back, and the texture of its side. Explain that the quarter will be changing its look soon. Tell them that you are going to play a guessing game with them. Have a volunteer sit in a chair facing the class. Blindfold the child. Explain that you are going to give her or him a piece of money, and that it will either be a quarter, or not a quarter. Explain that it could be another coin, or an object that is not a coin. Challenge children to carefully feel the front and back and texture of the sides to tell if it's a quarter or not. Rotate volunteers until all interested children have had a turn. Then question children about their knowledge of the quarter.

## Develop Oral Language

nonverbal prompt for active participation

• Preproduction: *Show us* (Point to class and self.) *which coin is a quarter.* (Present a quarter, dime, and penny from which to choose.) *Show us what the side of a quarter feels like.* (Model gestures for smooth and bumpy.)

one- or two-word response prompt

• Early production: *Can you tell me how many cents a quarter is worth? Can you tell me one thing about what a quarter looks like? Can you show me with the other coins if the quarter is bigger or smaller? Have you ever had a quarter of your own?*

prompt for short answers to higher-level thinking skills

• Speech emergence: *Do you know how many quarters are in a dollar? Do you know whose picture is on the front of a quarter?*

prompt for detailed answers to higher-level thinking skills

• Intermediate fluency: *Do you know what material is used to make the quarter? If you had a quarter, what would you do with it? What other kinds of money might be worth about as much as a quarter?*

# Guided Reading

## Preview and Predict

Tell children that the article they will read tells about the quarter and how it is changing. Ask children to raise their hands if they have a quarter or have ever seen one. Lead children on a picture walk to emphasize the concept of the changing quarter. Have them look carefully at the illustrations as you pose the following questions: *What does the picture on page 372 show? What do the quarters on page 373 show on them? How are these coins the same and different from one another? What kinds of coins are shown on page 374? Have you ever seen them before? Where do you think they come from?*

**GRAPHIC ORGANIZER**
Blackline Master 71

## Objectives

• To practice identifying cause and effect
• To reinforce understanding of main events
• To support working cooperatively

## Materials

One copy of Blackline Master 71 per child; pencils; child copy of *Change for the Quarter*

Go over the chart with children, explaining the column headings and the types of information each column should hold. (event from selection; effect of event) Discuss cause and effect links using a physical demonstration such as turning on or off the lights. Then fill in the top two boxes together. Have children help by volunteering facts to fit in the boxes as you read the selection together. Children can work individually or in pairs, where one child is completing the organizer with words and the other with pictures.

Have pairs of children use their completed Cause and Effect charts to quiz each other. As one child covers either the cause or effect, the other child should read the box that is visible and try to supply the missing cause or effect.

# III. BUILD SKILLS
## Comprehension

**REVIEW CAUSE AND EFFECT**
Blackline Master 72

**Alternate Teaching Strategy**
Teacher's Edition p. T69

### Objectives
- To recognize and identify a cause and effect relationship
- To reinforce critical thinking
- To reinforce hands-on learning

### Materials

One copy of Blackline Master 72 per child; scissors; construction paper; paste or glue

Go over the page with children. Explain that sometimes an effect can become a cause. (You might demonstrate with dominos or playing cards.) Tell children that picture number 1 is the first thing that happens. Have them cut out the square containing picture 1 and then paste it at the top of the construction paper. You may need to explain that the girl in picture 1 is throwing the ball to the boy. Have them find the picture of the boy. Ask: *What happens after the boy throws the ball behind his head?* Challenge them to find the picture that shows what happens next. Tell children to look carefully at the remaining pictures to complete the sequence of causes and effects.

**INFORMAL ASSESSMENT**

Direct children back to page 374. Ask a volunteer to tell what will happen if people save and collect the new quarters rather than spending them. (The government will make money.)

## Comprehension

**REVIEW FANTASY AND REALITY**
Blackline Master 73

**Alternate Teaching Strategy**
Teacher's Edition p. T66

### Objectives
- To recognize the difference between fantasy and reality
- To practice following directions

### Materials

One copy of Blackline Master 73 per child; circle shaped counters with an *R* on one side and an *M* on the other (one per pair of children); penny or playing marker (one per child)

Demonstrate the game with a volunteer and use pantomime as needed to clarify the rules. Each player takes a turn flipping the counter. If it lands with the *R* side facing up, that player moves her or his marker to the next square that shows a realistic character. If it lands with the *M* side facing up, the player should move the marker to the next square that shows a make-believe character. The first child to the castle wins the challenge!

**INFORMAL ASSESSMENT**

Refer children back to the article. Ask a volunteer to tell what real person is honored on the quarter. (George Washington)

## Vocabulary Strategy

**REVIEW SYNONYMS**
Blackline Master 74

**Alternate Teaching Strategy**
Teacher's Edition p. T71

### Objectives
• To recognize and understand synonyms
• To practice following directions

### Materials

One copy of Blackline Master 74 per child; pencils

Explain to children that the first word of each pair is spelled correctly. Read each word aloud with children. Then explain that the second word in each pair has scrambled letters. Direct them to unscramble the letters to make a word that means almost the same thing as the word next to the number. If children have difficulty, you may write the words on the board in random order. Pair children as needed according to fluency levels.

**INFORMAL ASSESSMENT**

Direct children back to article page 373. Have them find and say a word that means the same thing as created. (made)

## Vocabulary Strategy

**REVIEW CONTEXT CLUES**
Blackline Master 75
**Alternate Teaching Strategy**
Teacher's Edition p. T67

### Objectives
• To review using word order clues to define unfamiliar words
• To practice word identification
• To develop critical thinking

### Materials

One copy of Blackline Master 75 per child; pencils

Go over page with children. Read each sentence and discuss its meaning. Highlight each underlined word and review its role in the sentence. For example, say: *Look at the second picture. The underlined word comes after the word* He. *The word probably tells what he does.* Explain that looking at clues in the pictures is also a good way to figure out the meanings of unfamiliar words. Direct children to choose the darkened word that means almost the same thing as the underlined word. Tell them to circle the correct word.

**Informal Assessment**

Direct children back to page 373. Have them locate and read the following sentences: The eagle on the back side is going away. In its place, there will be 50 new designs. Ask a volunteer to use context clues to tell what the word *designs* means.

# Cause and Effect

**What Caused it to Happen?**

**What Happened?**

# One Thing After Another

**I.**

Name _____ Date _____

# Going from Real to Make-Believe

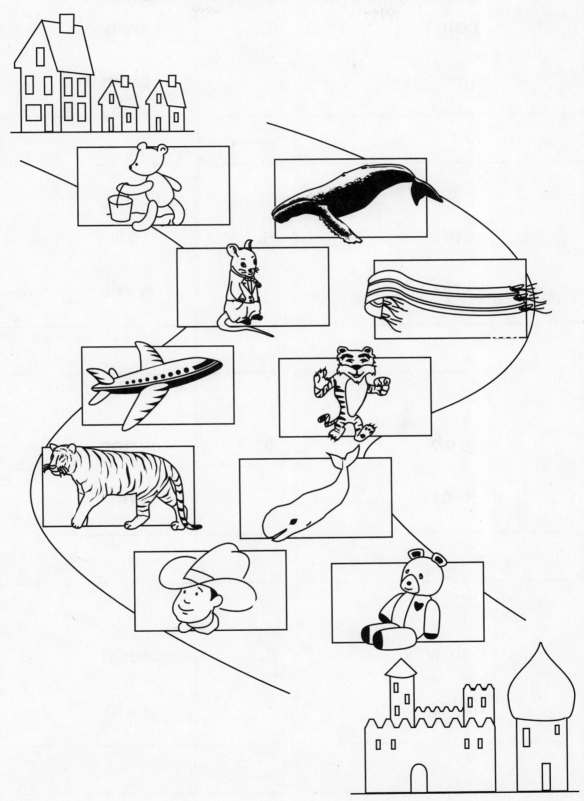

# Jumble Fun

1.      **coins**

        **ahencg**

_____

_____

2.      **own**

        **aevh**

_____

_____

3.      **date**

        **yda**

_____

_____

4.      **all**

        **rvyee**

_____

_____

5.      **grab**

        **keat**

_____

_____

6.      **stripe**

        **enli**

_____

_____

7.      **below**

        **drune**

_____

_____

8.      **world**

        **reath**

_____

_____

# What Does It Mean?

Sam is <u>prepared</u> to talk about his coins. He knows what he will say.

**ready**　　**next**　　**easy**

He <u>displays</u> his coins to the class.

**money**　　**shows**　　**sends**

"I like this one," he <u>stated</u>.

**said**　　**best**　　**pointed**

They <u>enjoyed</u> hearing his talk.

**class**　　**liked**　　**good**

# CHARLIE ANDERSON pp. 12A–43R

Written by Barbara Abercrombie Illustrated by Mark Graham

## BUILD BACKGROUND FOR LANGUAGE SUPPORT

## I. FOCUS ON READING

### Focus on Skills

### Develop Phonological Awareness

**OBJECTIVE:** Listen for /ủ/

**Alternate Teaching Strategy**
Teacher's Edition p. T64

Write the word *book* on the chalkboard. Make the /ủ/ sound for children and have them repeat the word after you. Ask if they know any words that rhyme with book (look, cook, shook). Tell children you are going to read the poem "The Neighborhood Book." Ask them to hold up a book every time they hear *book* or a word that rhymes with *book.*

**TPR**

## II. READ THE LITERATURE

### Vocabulary

**VOCABULARY**
upstairs
clothes
middle
roof
offered
chocolate

Print the vocabulary words on the chalkboard. Say each word and have the children repeat after you. Do the following activities to develop vocabulary word meanings.

upstairs: Pantomime walking up steps and prompt children to guess what you are doing. Let children pantomime and say: *I am walking upstairs.*

clothes: Say: *I am putting on my _____.* Ask children to pretend they are putting on clothes.

middle: Ask three children to come and stand at the front of the room, then ask: *Who is standing in the middle?*

roof: Show children a picture of a house and ask them to point to the roof of the house.

offered and chocolate: If possible, bring in chocolate chip cookies and give one to each child. Say: I *offered a cookie to you, and now I want you to show me where the chocolate is in the cookie.* Have each child point to the chocolate chips, before they eat the cookies.

**CONCEPT**
characteristics of cats

### Evaluate Prior Knowledge

If possible, bring a real cat into the classroom. Otherwise, use picture books and audio-visual materials that describe the habits of house cats. You may want to develop a bulletin board about cats and add to it as children complete their discussion about cats. For the center of the bulletin board, make a cat out of fake fur, textured fabric, or felt. Use felt for the ears, eyes, mouth, and tongue. Cut claws from a plastic milk bottle and color them with a black marker. Use broom bristles for whiskers. You may want to label the body parts. Around the center picture, group pictures of cats' foods, actions, habitats, and behaviors. The bulletin board will resemble a web when it is completed.

Have children bring in or make drawings and pictures of cats, and toy cats. Invite them to show what they brought and share their experiences with cats.

### Develop Oral Language

Invite children to demonstrate or pantomime a physical activity they've seen a cat perform. Children may work individually or in pairs to brainstorm scenes based on those observed or discussed earlier.

nonverbal prompt for active participation

• Preproduction: *Show us* (point to class and self) *how a cat moves. Offer possible responses: I see that a cat arches its back when it is angry.* Then model additional commands, such as: *Show us a sound a cat makes.*

one- or two-word response prompt

• Early production: *Do you have a cat? Would you like a cat? Do cats seem friendly? What color cats do you like?*

prompt for short answers to higher-level thinking skills

• Speech emergence: *Do you know what baby cats are called? How do cats scratch themselves? What do you think cats like to play with?*

prompt for detailed answers to higher-level thinking skills

• Intermediate fluency: *Why do you think cats rub against your leg? Do you know the kinds of things cats like to eat? What is something you'd like to know about cats?*

## Guided Reading

### Preview and Predict

Take children on a picture walk through *Charlie Anderson*. Tell children that this story is about a cat whose family is special and interesting. Use the story illustrations to establish characters and reinforce the concept of cats and cat behaviors. Then ask children to look carefully at the story pictures. Ask questions such as the following: *What color is the cat? What does the cat like to do at night? What is the cat doing on this page? How old do you think the girls are? What do they do for Charlie? How do the girls look on this page? What do you think happened? Who do you think the cat belongs to? Why?*

### Objectives

**GRAPHIC ORGANIZER**
Blackline Master 76

• To reinforce story elements and build comprehension
• To support hands-on learning
• To reinforce critical and creative thinking

### Materials

One copy of Blackline Master 76 per child; crayons or colored pencils; scissors; drawing paper; paste or glue; craft sticks; child copy of *Charlie Anderson.*

Invite children to color the character pictures. Have them cut out and paste each picture to a craft stick. As you read the story, invite children to use their puppets to show what is happening in each scene.

# III. BUILD SKILLS
## Phonics and Decoding

**REVIEW VARIANT VOWEL**
**/u̇/ *oo***
Blackline Master 77

**Alternate Teaching Strategy**
Teacher's Edition p. T64

**INFORMAL ASSESSMENT**

### Objectives
- To identify the /u̇/ *oo*
- To decode and read words with /u̇/ *oo*
- To practice following directions

### Materials
One copy of Blackline Master 77 per child; pencils

Together, read aloud the words providing a brief demonstration of each word's meaning. Instruct the children to draw a line connecting each picture with the correct word label. Ask children to write the correct word underneath the picture.

To assess recognition of words with the variant vowel /u̇/ *oo*, direct children back to the story text, for example, to page 22. Tell them to search the page carefully for words with the *oo* sound. *(woods)* Repeat using other pages from the story text. Call on teams to choose a page number for another team to search.

## Phonics and Decoding

**REVIEW VARIANT VOWEL**
**/u̇/ *oo***
Blackline Master 78

**Alternate Teaching Strategy**
Teacher's Edition p. T64

**INFORMAL ASSESSMENT**

### Objectives
- To review /u̇/ *oo*
- To practice following directions
- To reinforce using context clues

### Materials
One copy of Blackline Master 78 per child; pencils; colored pencils or crayons

Direct children's attention to the word box at the top of the page. Read the words together. Then read the sentences aloud together. Ask children to complete each sentence with the appropriate word from the word box. Invite them to draw a picture that shows what the sentence says.

Ask children to turn to page 18 of the text. Read aloud the sentence, *Every morning Charlie disappeared into the woods again.* Ask them to identify which word has the /u̇/ sound (woods) and to draw an illustration described by the sentence.

# Comprehension

**INTRODUCE DRAWING
CONCLUSIONS**
Blackline Master 79

**Alternate Teaching Strategy**
Teacher's Edition p. T66

**Objectives**
• To practice drawing conclusions
• To encourage critical thinking

**Materials**
One copy of Blackline Master 79 per child; pencils; child copy of *Charlie Anderson*

Identify the three areas on the page and explain that these people represent the different people that care for Charlie Anderson. Discuss the fact that each group of people calls the cat by a different name. Help children write the name that each group of people called the cat in the bubble. Allow children to use their books as reference. Help children draw the conclusion that the final name, Charlie Anderson, was made by combining the first two names, Charlie and Anderson.

**INFORMAL ASSESSMENT**

Refer children back to *Charlie Anderson*. Ask them questions based on the illustrations, such as, *Look at the illustration on page 21. Why do you think Sarah is dressing him up? Do you think he likes it?*

# Vocabulary Strategy

**INTRODUCE ANTONYMS**
Blackline Master 80

**Alternate Teaching Strategy**
Teacher's Edition p. T67

**Objectives**
• To practice recognition of opposites
• To practice following directions

**Materials**
One copy of Blackline Master 80 per child

Tell them that the pictures on the left side of the page (point to the left side of children's papers) have an opposite picture on the right. Instruct them to connect the opposite pairs with a line. When pictures are connected, have children work in pairs to discuss which pictures they joined and why.

**INFORMAL ASSESSMENT**

Direct children back to the text. Tell them to turn to page 23 and find a word on the page that means the opposite of *quiet*. Then have them identify the word *fatter* on the same page, and ask them to find the opposite. Children may practice using opposites by prompting searches with each other.

Name _____ Date _____

# Story Puppets

# Picture-Word Matching

**looked**

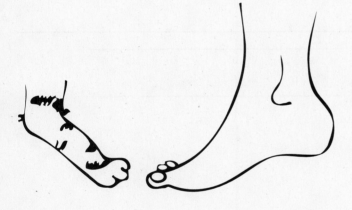

**cookie**

**foot**

# Moments with Charlie Anderson

| woods | foot | cookies |
|---|---|---|

_____

Charlie sleeps at the _____ of my bed.

_____

_____

We were too worried to eat _____.

_____

_____

Is Charlie in the _____?

# What's His Name?

# Finding Opposites

**short**

**dry**

**wet**

**tall**

**day**

**night**

# FERNANDO'S GIFT pp. 44A–67R

Written and Photographed by Douglas Keister

## BUILD BACKGROUND FOR LANGUAGE SUPPORT

## I. FOCUS ON READING

### Focus on Skills

**OBJECTIVE:** Listen for soft *c* and soft *g*

**Alternate Teaching Strategy**
Teacher's Edition p. T68

**TPR**
Use body language and physical response to act out each word choice.

### Develop Phonological Awareness

Read aloud the poem "My Gifts." Read the first line again, and ask children to listen for the word that ends with the /s/ sound. *(mice)* Have children slowly say the word *mice.* Then say the following sentence and word pairs. Each time, have children say the word that ends with the same /s/ sound as in the word *mice. Mom gave me* (money/rice; ice/water; lace/fish; juice/fruit).

Say the word *cage*, emphasizing the sound /j/. Repeat the activity, using the word pairs that follow. *Mom gave me (a)* (page/part; home/change; bandage/mask).

## II. READ THE LITERATURE

**VOCABULARY**
village
noisy
diving
explained
soil
harm

### Vocabulary

Print the vocabulary words on the chalkboard. Demonstrate the definition of each word, using verbal explanation as well as physical movement.

village: Show children a picture of a small town and ask them what they see. If they say *town,* explain that another word for a place where people live is a *village.* Ask them to name things they might find in a village by saying: *You might find a_____* (store, school, etc.) *in a village.*

noisy: Have two children come forward. Ask one child to whisper his name to the class and the other child to shout his or her name. Ask: *Who is being noisy?* Have children respond by saying, for example: *Maria is being noisy.*

diving: Pantomime diving into a pool and swimming. Invite other children to dive into the pretend pool. But first they must say: *I am diving into the pool!*

explained: Give simple instructions for planting a seed. Then write on the board: *The teacher explained how to plant a seed.* Invite children to explain something they know how to do.

soil: Refer to your instructions for planting a seed. Say: *We dig a hole in the _____.* Have children fill in the missing word and repeat the sentence.

harm: Say: *If you don't water your plant you could _____ it.* To check for understanding, ask what could happen to the plant if it is harmed.

### Evaluate Prior Knowledge

**CONCEPT**
protecting the environment

Display a variety of photos or illustrations of mountains, oceans, forests, cities, farmland, and suburbs. Tell children that the environment means Earth and everything on it. Protecting the environment means helping keep Earth safe and clean. Name some things and show pictures of things that hurt our environment, including exhaust from cars, litter, and ocean debris. Discuss with children what people can do to help the environment.

### Develop Oral Language

Lead the class on a "Clean Our Environment" walk around the interior and exterior of the school grounds. As you walk, have them come up with a plan for protecting different areas in their school environment. If possible, allow time for children to enact their plan.

nonverbal prompt for active participation

- Preproduction: *Show us* (point to class and self) *how you feel (*point to your face) *when you see trash in your school.*

one- or two-word response prompt

- Early production: *Have you ever helped clean up in this way before? Where or what did you clean up?*

prompt for short answers to higher-level thinking skills

- Speech emergence: *Who else could help us clean up the school? How could they help? What could we do with all the trash we found?*

prompt for detailed answers to higher-level thinking skills

- Intermediate fluency: *How does it make you feel to make our environment more beautiful? What else could we do as a class?*

## Guided Reading

### Preview and Predict

Tell children that this story is about a boy who wants to give a special friend a present for her birthday. Ask: *What do you suppose he will give to her?* The story also tells about the life of a real boy who lives in the rainforest. Ask: *What do you think his life is like?* Lead children on a picture walk through the text to reinforce the concept of protecting our environment. Pose questions such as the following, calling on volunteers for verbal or physical responses: *What can you tell about the place Fernando lives? Who does Fernando live with? What kinds of things does his family do? Can you find Fernando's special friend? What can you tell about her? What gift do you think Fernando will give to her? How might that gift help protect the environment?*

**GRAPHIC ORGANIZER**
Blackline Master 81

### Objectives
- To reinforce the ability to draw conclusions
- To reinforce working together cooperatively

### Materials

One copy of Blackline Master 81 per child; pencils; child copy of *Fernando's Gift*

Review the page with children, using an example from the story to explain the headings *Clues* and *Conclusions*. For example, show the picture on the cover, and point to *Clue*. Then say, *Fernando can ride a horse,* and point to *Conclusion*. Then have children look at other pictures and read or listen to the story to find other clues and reach other conclusions. Children needing language support may draw their responses and use one- or two-word labels. Have children use the chart to explain or act out their clues and conclusions.

# III. BUILD SKILLS
## Phonics and Decoding

**REVIEW SOFT *c* AND SOFT *g***

Blackline Master 82

**Alternate Teaching Strategy**
Teacher's Edition p. T68

**INFORMAL ASSESSMENT**

### Objectives
• To identify words with soft *c* and soft *g* sounds
• To match pictures with vocabulary
• To practice following directions

### Materials
One copy of Blackline Master 82 per child; pencils

Direct children's attention to the box containing vocabulary words at the top of the page. Read the words aloud with children, stressing the soft *c* and soft *g* sounds. Tell children to look at the pictures and discuss what they see. Have them write each vocabulary word below its matching picture.

To evaluate children's ability to recognize sounds, have them locate and read on page 53, the word with the soft *c* sound. *(place)* Then have them locate and read on page 54, the word with the soft *g* sound. *(village)*

## Phonics and Decoding

**REVIEW SOFT *c*, SOFT *g*, AND /ù/**

Blackline Master 83

**Alternate Teaching Strategy**
Teacher's Edition p. T68

**INFORMAL ASSESSMENT**

### Objectives
• To identify soft *c* and soft *g* sounds
• To blend and read words with soft *c* and soft *g* sounds
• To review words with the /ù/ *oo* sound

### Materials
One copy of Blackline Master 83 per child; colored pencils or crayons; scissors; glue or paste

Help children decode and read the words in the box at the top of the page. Direct them to cut out the vocabulary words along the dotted lines. Model how to match each word label to the correct picture. Instruct children to paste the correct word in the box near remaining corresponding pictures.

Invite children to find the words *roof, rice, village, age,* and *woods* in the story *Fernando's Gift*. When children find each word, have them read aloud the sentence containing it. (*roof*, p. 48; *rice*, p. 51; *village*, p. 54; *age*, p. 57; *wood*, p. 48)

# Comprehension

**INTRODUCE COMPARE AND CONTRAST**
Blackline Master 84

**Alternate Teaching Strategy**
Teacher's Edition p. T69

## Objectives
• To compare and contrast personal surroundings with story settings
• To reinforce critical thinking
• To practice following directions

## Materials
One copy of Blackline Master 84 per child; colored pencils or crayons; child copy of *Fernando's Gift*

Use words and body language (pointing to self and story illustrations, for example) to explain that the boxes on the left pertain to Fernando's life, and the boxes on the right ask children something about their own lives. Read the picture labels with children. Have children draw their responses in the boxes. One- or two-word labels may be added.

**INFORMAL ASSESSMENT**

Tell children to look at the illustrations in *Fernando's Gift*. Direct them to search for something that is the same and different about Fernando's family and their own.

# Vocabulary Strategy

**REVIEW ANTONYMS**
Blackline Master 85

**Alternate Teaching Strategy**
Teacher's Edition p. T67

## Objectives
• To identify antonym pairs
• To practice word identification
• To practice following directions

## Materials

One copy of Blackline Master 85 per child; colored pencils or crayons; glue or paste; scissors

Direct children's attention to the word boxes at the top of the page. Have them color the pictures. Model one pair with body language or physical examples. Explain that the word pairs are opposites. Tell children to cut out the words and paste each under the correct picture. Have children work with a partner to demonstrate the opposite word pairs.

**INFORMAL ASSESSMENT**

Have children refer back to the story text. Tell them to look at the words on page 48 and search for a word that means the opposite of *day*. Write *day* on the chalkboard. When the word has been identified, write *night* next to it. Have children take turns creating "opposite hunts".

Name _____ Date _____

| Clues | Conclusions |
|-------|-------------|
|       |             |

# Name the Pictures

| place | village | rice | age |
|---|---|---|---|

_____

_____

_____

_____

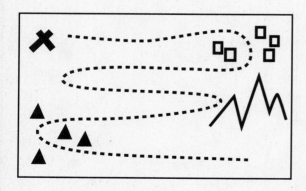

_____

_____

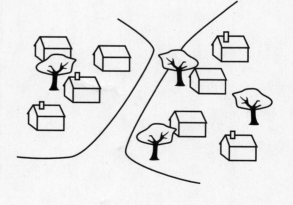

_____

_____

# Name What You See

| path | roof | rice |
|------|------|------|
| woods | village | age |

# Different Worlds

Fernando's home is like this.

How is mine the same?

Fernando's school is like this.

How is mine different?

# Finding Opposites

| big | full | dry |
|-----|------|-----|
| empty | small | wet |

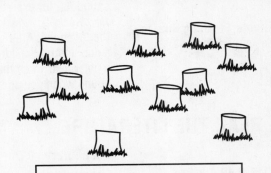

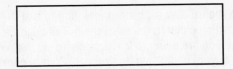

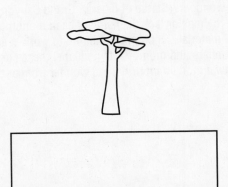

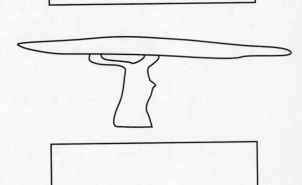

# THE BEST VACATION EVER pp. 68A–91R

Written by Diane Hoyt-Goldsmith  Illustrated by Cecily Lang

## BUILD BACKGROUND FOR LANGUAGE SUPPORT

## I. FOCUS ON READING

### Focus on Skills

**OBJECTIVE:** Listen for /ô/

**Alternate Teaching Strategy**
Teacher's Edition p. T70

**TPR**

### Develop Phonological Awareness

Make the sound of /ô/ for children. Give some examples of words containing the sound /ô/, for example, jaw, talk, haunch. Then say word pairs such as *law/bag, flaw/week, bowl/saw*. Have children raise their hands when they hear the word with the /ô/ sound. After several children have responded, read the poem "City Zoo" aloud. Instruct children to listen closely for words with the /ô/ sound and to roar like a polar bear when these words are read. Read the poem slowly and stress the /ô/ sound when you come to words such as *saw, paw, claw, jaw,* and *macaw*.

## II. READ THE LITERATURE

**VOCABULARY**
vacation
museum
wonder
guess
brave
practiced

### Vocabulary

List the vocabulary words on the chalkboard. Say each word, pointing to it at the same time. Pronounce them again, inviting children to repeat them. Tell children that you are going to tell them a story, and you are going to leave some words out. When omitting a word, clap to indicate that a word is missing. Instruct children to come to the board and identify the word they think would make sense in the story. Possibilities might include: *My mom just told me that we are going on a* (vacation). *I* (wonder) *where we are going. One* (guess) *I have is to the ocean. I am afraid of water because I can't swim too well. I must be* (brave). *Maybe if I* (practiced) *my swimming I wouldn't be afraid. I hope we're also going to look at old things in a* (museum). Go to the Discuss Meanings section and answer each question using physical modeling or photo props, then have children answer the question.

**CONCEPT**
historical sites and natural
wonders in the United States

### Evaluate Prior Knowledge

Gather sources from the library (travel books/magazines, encyclopedias) that contain pictures of monuments and natural wonders such as lakes, oceans, and mountains. Explain to children that the United States has many beautiful and special places to visit. Post a map on the chalkboard. Show pictures of a few very familiar wonders, such as the Statue of Liberty, the Grand Canyon, and one of the Great Lakes. Show pictures and read or tell about a few wonders. (Statue of Liberty, Grand Canyon, Pacific Ocean) Help volunteers correctly tape or tack the name of each monument near its location. Using the reference materials, encourage children to work in appropriate fluency pairs to find natural wonders and monuments and label these correctly on the map. Also, ask children to draw a monument or natural wonder from another country they know well.

## Develop Oral Language

nonverbal prompt for active
participation

- Preproduction: *Show us* (point to class and self) *a picture of a monument or wonder you think is really special. Show us where it belongs on the map.* Use arm gestures to indicate the map and picture resources.

one- or two-word response
prompt

- Early production: *What is this famous monument called?* Display a picture of the Statue of Liberty. *What is she holding? Can you tell me one thing about any of the other monuments? Which monument would you like to visit?*

prompt for short answers to
higher-level thinking skills

- Speech emergence: *What is the name of this famous natural wonder?* Show a picture of the Grand Canyon. *What is it made of? How could you get to the bottom? What are the names of the monuments/natural wonders you have added to the map? Why are they special? Were they made by people or by nature? How can you tell?*

prompt for detailed answers
to higher-level thinking skills

- Intermediate fluency: *Have you ever been to see one of these special places? Have you been to any other famous places in the United States? Tell us about famous places like this in other countries.*

# Guided Reading

## Preview and Predict

Ask children if they have ever been on a trip. Tell children that this story is about a girl named Amanda who tells a friend all about her vacation trip through a series of letters. Pair English-speaking children with those needing additional language support. Lead children on a picture walk using the story and illustrations to reinforce the concept of historical sites and natural wonders in the United States. Have one child answer the questions as the other child records responses on paper. Ask questions such as: *How old do you think Amanda is? Where do you think she is going in this picture? How do you think Amanda feels about her vacation? How can you tell? What type of place do you think Amanda and her family are visiting in this picture?*

## Objectives

- To practice comparing and contrasting story elements
- To support understanding of main events and story details
- To develop understanding of character personality traits
- To encourage creative and critical thinking

**GRAPHIC ORGANIZER**
Blackline Master 86

## Materials

One copy of Blackline Master 86 per child; pencils, colored pencils, or crayons; child copy of *The Best Vacation Ever.*

Go over the page with children and clarify the three different category activities. Tell children that this sheet will help them keep track of Amanda's trip and her family's responses to each place they visit. Have children complete the chart with text or pictures as fluency levels dictate. Ask for one- or two-word labels with the illustrations. Demonstrate the first vacation stop for children, writing *Kitty Hawk, North Carolina* in the *Place* column. Discuss how Amanda and Sammy react to Kitty Hawk and then help children record these reactions in the appropriate columns. Have children add other entries as the class reads the story together. Have children find one place where Amanda and Sammy had similar reactions, and one place they reacted differently.

# III. BUILD SKILLS
## Phonics and Decoding

**REVIEW /ô/ *aw, au, a***
Blackline Master 87

### Objectives
- To practice identifying words with the sound /ô/ *aw, au, a*
- To extend understanding through creative storytelling

**Alternate Teaching Strategy**
Teacher's Edition p. T70

### Materials
One copy of Blackline Master 87 per child; scissors; construction paper or tag board; glue or paste

Go over the page with children. Have children name each picture and match it to the correct word on the left. Have children cut out the words then help them glue or paste both words and pictures onto construction paper or tag board. Encourage children to create stories with the words, using the pictures as illustrations.

**INFORMAL ASSESSMENT**

Have children look at the story illustrations and text to find a word containing /ô/. (hawk, astronaut, walk)

## Phonics and Decoding

**REVIEW /ô/ *aw, au, a; soft c, g;* /ù/ *oo***
Blackline Master 88

### Objectives
- To review the sounds /ô/ *aw, au, a;* /s/ *ce;* /j/ *ge;* /ù/ *oo*
- To work cooperatively
- To practice following directions

**Alternate Teaching Strategy**
Teacher's Edition p. T64, T68, T70

### Materials
One copy of Blackline Master 88 per child; colored pencils or crayons; scissors

Go over the page with children. Use *hawk* to demonstrate matching the word/picture pairs. Have children cut out the squares. Help them match each word square to its picture/word square partner. Children can then work in pairs to organize their picture/word cards by common sounds.

**INFORMAL ASSESSMENT**

Play a Seek and Find game. List various words from the story text that contain the focus sounds. *(astronaut, restaurants, huge)* Ask children to find the words in their text. Then ask children to tell which sound the word contains. Slowly make the letter sounds for them if necessary.

## Comprehension

**DRAW CONCLUSIONS**
Blackline Master 89

### Objectives
- To use information to draw conclusions
- To reinforce following directions
- To extend the story

**Alternate Teaching Strategy**
Teacher's Edition p. T66

### Materials
One copy of Blackline Master 89 per child; colored pencils or crayons

Go over the page with children. Tell children that the box with the picture in it tells something about Amanda. Read the first one for them. Tell them that they will play detective to answer the question on the top, *What does Amanda want to be?* Ask them to look closely at the picture clues and the words to answer the question. Pair children needing language support with fluent children. Encourage them to write or draw their responses, and use one- to two-word labels if possible.

**INFORMAL ASSESSMENT**   Direct children back to the story text and illustration on pages 74–75. Discuss the pictures of Orville Wright flying the first airplane at Kitty Hawk. Tell children that Amanda loves planes. Ask them: *What do you think Amanda might want to be that day?* (a pilot or inventor) Have children take turns finding pictures and asking each other this question.

## Vocabulary Strategy

**REVIEW *-er, -est* ENDINGS**
Blackline Master 90

### Objectives
• To practice reading words with inflectional endings *-er and -est*
• To practice following directions
• To reinforce hands-on learning

**Alternate Teaching Strategy**
Teacher's Edition p. T71

### Materials

One copy of Blackline Master 90 per child; scissors; glue or paste

Tell children that they are going to put things in a special order. Tell them that each word at the top of the page describes one of the pictures at the bottom of the page. Read aloud the words with children. Have them cut out the words on the top of the page and place each with the correct picture below.

**INFORMAL ASSESSMENT**   Direct children back to the text. Locate a word from the story, such as *cold* on page 74. Say and write the word on the chalkboard. Ask children to supply the *-er* and *-est* forms of the word.

Name_____ Date_____

# A Trip Log

| | Place |
|---|---|
| | |

| | Amanda's Reactions |
|---|---|
| | |

| | Sammy's Reactions |
|---|---|
| | |

# Give the Pictures Names

astronaut

hawk

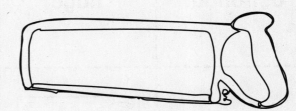

saw

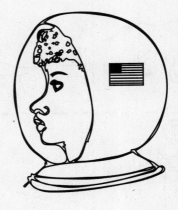

Name _____ Date _____

# Word and Picture Match

| hawk | large | place | foot |
|------|-------|-------|------|
| book | practice | partridge | saw |
| astronaut | huge | look | took |

# What Does Amanda Want to Be?

Amanda loves country music.

Amanda thinks park rangers are nice.

Amanda makes a photo scrapbook.

Name _____ Date _____

# Long, Bigger, Largest!

| long | longer | longest |
|------|--------|---------|
| large | larger | largest |
| big | bigger | biggest |

MISSISSIPPI RIVER

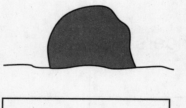

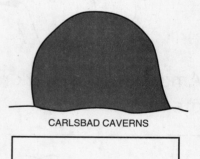

CARLSBAD CAVERNS

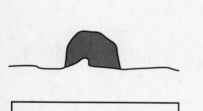

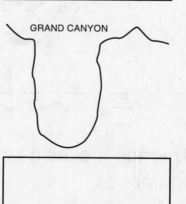

GRAND CANYON

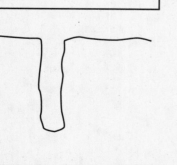

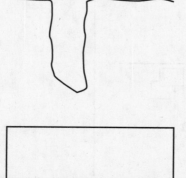

Grade 2

# ZIPPING, ZAPPING, ZOOMING BATS pp. 92A–115R

Written by Ann Earle  Illustrated by Henry Cole

## BUILD BACKGROUND FOR LANGUAGE SUPPORT

## I. FOCUS ON READING

### Focus on Skills

### Develop Phonological Awareness

**OBJECTIVE:** Listen for Digraphs *ph* and *tch*

**TPR**

Prepare slips of paper numbered 1–5 with the following word parts on them: 1.*graph*, 2. *phones*, 3. *tch*, 4. *tch*, 5. *tch*. Distribute the slips to five volunteers. Then prepare five other numbered slips with following word parts: 1. *photo*, 2. *tele*, 3. *pi*, 4. *i*,  5. *ca*. Keep them for your own use. Explain that you will say the beginning part of a word and the number of the slip. Tell the child holding that numbered slip to bring her slip to you. Say the sound on the slip. Instruct children to repeat the sound and the completed word. Read together the poem "Questions About Bats," and have children stand up when they hear these sounds.

## II. READ THE LITERATURE

### Vocabulary

**VOCABULARY**
explore
fact
disturb
nature
object
several

Say each word while printing it on the chalkboard. Use each word in a sentence, saying the sentence slowly. Organize the class into groups of 3 to 4 children. Assign each group a sentence. Have them come to a group decision as to the meaning of each underlined word. Invite them to demonstrate and pantomime the meanings of the sentences.

Use the following sentences:

*It is a* <u>fact</u> *that bats can fly.*

*When people* <u>explore</u> *caves, the bats often fly away.*

*Sometimes people* <u>disturb</u> *caves filled with baby bats.*

*Many people enjoy visiting* <u>nature</u> *centers to learn about animals and plants.*

*Bats use sound waves to fly around an* <u>object</u>.

*There are* <u>several</u> *kinds of bats. Many eat insects like mosquitoes.*

Ask the class to guess the meaning of the word as acted out by each group.  Have each group explain how they came up with the definition they acted out.

### Evaluate Prior Knowledge

**CONCEPT**
nocturnal animals

Discuss basic animal activities. (finding food, caring for young, creating safe shelter) Ask children to suggest information about animal habits. Explain that nocturnal animals perform these activities at night. Show pictures of nocturnal animals, such as owls, opossums, raccoons, and bats. Assign one half of the class to role-play things in nature that stay still or sleep at night. Assign the other half of the class to role-play actions of nocturnal animals at night.

If possible, turn off all or part of the classroom lights. As children act out their roles, narrate the scene: *It is night in the forest. The trees are still and the forest is very quiet and peaceful. It is time for the nocturnal animals to come out and hunt for food. They must be careful not to disturb sleeping animals. When they see their prey, they swoop down or pounce on it to catch and eat it.* Model some movements of nocturnal animals. (swooping, pouncing, stalking)

## Develop Oral Language

Question children about their role-playing.

nonverbal prompt for active participation

• Preproduction: *Are you a night creature or a sleeping part of nature? (*use pictures to indicate options) *Show us* (point to class and self) *what you do at night.* (point to night picture)

one- or two-word response prompt

• Early production: *Have you ever seen a bat or an owl?* (point to pictures) *What part of nature are you? Can you tell us one word about who/what you are? Do you make any sounds? Can you make those sounds?*

prompt for short answers to higher-level thinking skills

• Speech emergence: *What do you think the other part of nature* (point to other group) *experiences at night? Think about your role in the skit. Describe what you see around you.*

prompt for detailed answers to higher-level thinking skills

• Intermediate fluency: *What do you think is easy and difficult about being a nocturnal animal? Do you know what kinds of nocturnal animals live in your community? How might nocturnal animals be good for nature?*

# Guided Reading

### Preview and Predict

Tell children that this article tells about bats, which are nocturnal animals. Explain that the selection gives both interesting and surprising facts about bats and tells why bats should not seem scary. Lead children on a picture walk through the story. Ask questions based on the illustrations, pausing to reinforce the concept of nocturnal animals and allow children to predict and discuss. Pose questions such as: *What do you think this picture shows? How might this relate to bats? If bats are most active at night, how do you think they keep from running into things? Look at the close-up of the bat on page 102. What part of the bat do you think helps it swoop and fly so fast? How do you think bats use their claws? What do you think bats do during the winter months? Where do you suppose most bats live?*

### Objectives

**GRAPHIC ORGANIZER**
Blackline Master 91

• To reinforce recognition of story events
• To practice drawing conclusions
• To support cooperative learning

### Materials

One copy of Blackline Master 91 per child; pencils; child copy of *Zipping, Zapping, Zooming Bats*

Go over the chart with children. Explain the column heads and the type of information belonging in each column. Discuss and list possible types of facts about bats on the chalkboard, such as physical traits, hunting, or habits. Then invite children to highlight a detail in the text or illustration. Have them read, draw, or point to the data. Ask the class to draw a conclusion from the fact. Help children list both fact and conclusion in the chart. Pair children of varied fluencies to complete the chart. Allow pairs to use both writing and illustration.

Group different pairs together to share their charts and reinforce the skill of drawing conclusions. Have them read the facts and conclusions to each other. Challenge them to see if any different conclusions were drawn from the same set of facts.

# III. BUILD SKILLS

## Phonics and Decoding

**REVIEW DIGRAPHS *ph, tch***
Blackline Master 92

**Alternate Teaching Strategy**
Teacher's Edition p. T72

### Objectives
- To practice reading words with Digraphs *ph, tch*
- To review initial and final consonants
- To practice following directions

### Materials
One copy of Blackline Master 92 per child; scissors; paste or glue

Review the page with children, noticing the pictures and the empty box below each. Read the words in the boxes aloud, as well as the text below each picture. Have children cut out the words at the top. Tell children to choose a word from the boxes to complete the sentences.

**INFORMAL ASSESSMENT**

Direct children to page 97 to locate a /ch/ *tch* word. (catching) Print the word on the chalkboard. Ask a volunteer to pronounce and read this word in the sentence from the text.

## Phonics and Decoding

**REVIEW DIGRAPHS *ph, tch*; /ò/; *Soft c, g***
Blackline Master 93

**Alternate Teaching Strategy**
Teacher's Edition p. T68, T70, T72

### Objectives
- To review Digraphs *ph, tch*
- To review variant vowels
- To practice reading words with Soft *c, g*

### Materials
One copy of Blackline Master 93 per child; colored pencils or crayons; scissors; paste or glue

Tell children that the words in the boxes at the top of the page go with the pictures on the cave shape below. Read the words together if necessary. Have children cut out the words before matching each to the correct picture. Tell children to leave the cave opening empty, and to draw different features of caves in this space.

**INFORMAL ASSESSMENT**

Print the following words on the chalkboard: *pitched, bounce.* Tell children to hunt carefully on page 100 to find these words. Once they have located them, ask them to pronounce and read them in the text sentences.

## Comprehension

**COMPARE AND CONTRAST**
Blackline Master 94

**Alternate Teaching Strategy**
Teacher's Edition p. T69

### Objectives
- To compare and contrast familiar items
- To practice identifying similarities and differences

### Materials
One copy of Blackline master 94 per child; pencil, colored pencils or crayons

Direct children to look carefully at the pictures and then name what each picture shows. Model matching the picture of the bat wing with the picture of the hand. Have children draw a line to connect other matching pictures and tell why they connected each pair.

**INFORMAL ASSESSMENT**

Direct children's attention to the illustrations on pages 102 and 103. Ask volunteers to tell things that are the same and different about bats and birds.

## Vocabulary Strategy

**INFLECTIONAL ENDINGS**
Blackline Master 95

**Alternate Teaching Strategy**
Teacher's Edition p. T71

**INFORMAL ASSESSMENT**

### Objectives
• To reinforce reading words with inflectional endings
• To practice reading base words
• To practice following directions

### Materials

One copy of Blackline Master 95 per child; scissors; paste or glue

Read with children the words in the boxes and the sentences below each picture. Help them identify the base word. Direct children to cut out the words. Tell them to choose a word from the boxes to complete each sentence. Have children glue or paste the word into the sentence and then read the sentence aloud.

Ask children to look at the text on page 98. Ask volunteers to use the words *bigger* and *biggest* in a sentence to compare and contrast the eating habits of brown, gray, and free-tailed bats. (gray is bigger than brown; free-tailed is biggest)

Name _____ Date _____

# STORY DETAILS

| Facts | Conclusion |
|-------|------------|
|       |            |
|       |            |
|       |            |
|       |            |

# Phil Photographs a Hungry Bat

| catch | phantom |
|-------|---------|
| photo | high-pitched |

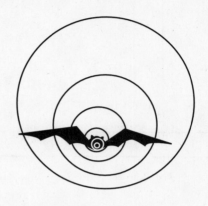

I thought the bat was a

[                    ] !

The bat makes a

[                    ] sound.

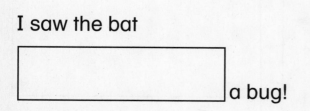

I saw the bat

[                ] a bug!

I will take a

[                ] of the bat!

# The World of Bats

| dodges | high-pitched | catch |
|--------|--------------|-------|
| entrances | Australia | photo |
|  | claws |  |

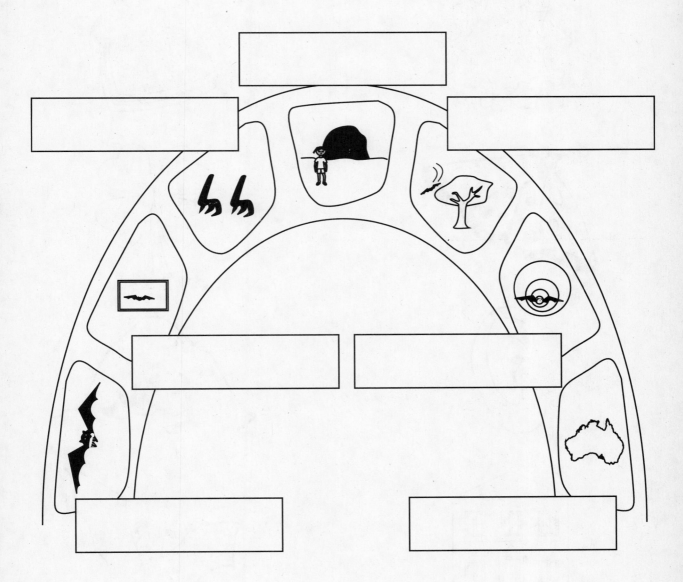

# Bats and Us

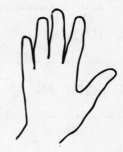

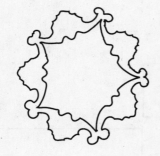

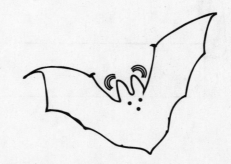

# Tiniest Bats, Largest Bats

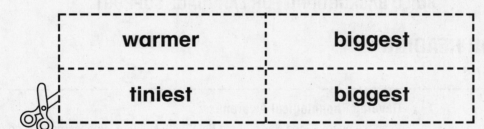

| warmer | biggest |
|--------|---------|
| tiniest | biggest |

The hog-nosed bat is the

_____ bat

in the world.

The flying fox is the

_____ bat

in the world.

Mexican free-tailed bats fly

south where it is

_____ .

The number of gray bats is

getting _____ .

# GOING BATTY FOR BATS pp. 116A–125R

Time For Kids

## BUILD BACKGROUND FOR LANGUAGE SUPPORT

## I. FOCUS ON READING
### Focus on Skills

**OBJECTIVE:** Review vowel and consonant sounds

**Alternate Teaching Strategy**
Teacher's Edition p. T64; p. T68; p.T70; p. T72

**TPR**

### Develop Phonological Awareness

Read the poem "Good News About Bats" with children, emphasizing the sounds covered in this unit, for example, *look (/ù/ oo); age (/j/ ge); mice (/s/ ce); awful (/ô/ aw); catch* (digraph tch)*; and phony* (digraph ph). Assign a color to each sound, and review this connection with children. Then pass out an assortment of crayons to children. Ask children to raise the corresponding colored crayon each time they hear a word containing that sound. Reread the poem, choosing one sound to emphasize. Repeat with each sound and its corresponding color.

## II. READ THE LITERATURE

**VOCABULARY**
darkness
scary
breath
study
crops
cover

### Vocabulary

Print the vocabulary words on the chalkboard. Read sentences from the story selection containing vocabulary words (*darkness*-p. 119, *scary*-p. 119, *breath*-p. 119, *crops*-p. 119, *study*-p.120, *cover*-p.121). Invite children to guess the meaning of each vocabulary word. Write children's suggestions on the chalkboard, and then reread each sentence with the suggested definitions. Organize the class into small groups and assign each a sentence with the suggested definition. Have the groups act out the new sentences. Discuss as a class which definition is the correct one.

### Evaluate Prior Knowledge

**CONCEPT**
bats help people

Show children pictures of bats. Then dramatize the concept of helping people by walking around the room and doing things to help the children, such as helping them straighten their desks, or tying their shoes, or helping a child put on her or his sweater or jacket. Invite children to guess what you are doing. (helping people) Repeat examples of helping people until children answer correctly. Explain that bats help people, also. Tell them that bats help by eating bugs and rodents that people don't like. Ask if anyone knows of a folk-tale or story that tells something scary about bats. Stress the fact that bats eat bugs and not people. Say: *Bats eat bugs; they don't bite people.* Show pictures of bats so children are able to see how they look and move.

## Develop Oral Language

Invite children to draw pictures of bats or people doing something helpful. Ask children to share any experiences, pleasant or otherwise, that they have had with bats.

nonverbal prompt for active participation

- Preproduction: *Show us* (point to class and self) *your picture. Show us what the bat (person, animal) is doing.*

one- or two-word response prompt

- Early production: *Have you ever seen a bat? Does your picture show a bat? Tell me a word that describes a bat.*

prompt for short answers to higher-level thinking skills

- Speech emergence: *What is the bat (or other creature) doing in your picture? Do bats scare you? Where do you think you could find a bat? What would you do if you saw one?*

prompt for detailed answers to higher-level thinking skills

- Intermediate fluency: *What kind of bugs do you think bats like to eat? What do you think a bat would do if it saw you? How is the bat (person, animal) in your picture helping someone?*

# Guided Reading

## Preview and Predict

Tell children that before they actually read the article, you're going to take a picture walk through the pages and try to answer some questions. Ask them to think of the things they know and think about bats while they look at the pictures. Ask questions such as: *What do you think this picture shows about bats? How do you think they move? Do they walk and run or fly? What color do you think they are? What kinds of things do you think they like to eat? Where do you think they live? Do people try to hurt them? Do bats try to hurt people?*

## Objectives

- To reinforce understanding of story details
- To support hands-on learning

**GRAPHIC ORGANIZER**
Blackline Master 96

## Materials

**Alternate Teaching Strategy**
Teacher's Edition p. T69

One copy of Blackline Master 96 per child; pencils, colored pencils, or crayons; child copy of *Going Batty for Bats*

Go over the Venn diagram with children, and explain that it will help them record information about two ideas: fears about bats and facts about bats. Point out that the two outer areas of the circles show how the ideas are different, and the section in the middle shows how they are alike. As they read the story, tell children to write or draw in the left-hand circle things that are scary about bats. They should write or draw in the right-hand circle things that are true about bats. Show children how to move entries that appear on both lists into the overlapping center section. Children may work in writing/drawing pairs as their fluency levels require.

Reinforce the skill of compare and contrast. Invite children to explain their Venn Diagrams to the class. Help children compare and contrast their diagrams. Is *everyone afraid of the same things?*

# III. BUILD SKILLS

## Comprehension

**COMPARE AND CONTRAST**
Blackline Master 97

**Alternate Teaching Strategy**
Teacher's Edition p. T69

**Objectives**
• To reinforce compare and contrast
• To reinforce understanding of inflectional endings
• To practice following directions

**Materials**
One copy of Blackline Master 97 per child; scissors

Go over the page with children. Write on the chalkboard the following words, explaining what each word means: *smallest, bigger, faster, safest.* Tell children to cut out the pieces along the dotted lines. Show them how to piece the rectangles together to form the words shown on the board. Instruct children to look carefully at the pictures in order to choose the correct pieces. Ask children to name one thing that is the same in each picture and one thing that is different.

**INFORMAL ASSESSMENT**

Refer back to the article text. Tell children to look carefully at page 119. Ask them to find one of the words they just built using Batty Words. Tell them that the word will tell what kind of helpers bats are. (biggest)

## Comprehension

**DRAW CONCLUSION**
Blackline Master 98

**Alternate Teaching Strategy**
Teacher's Edition p. T66, T71

**Objectives**
• To draw conclusions from the illustrations
• To practice word identification
• To reinforce story elements

**Materials**
One copy of Blackline Master 98 per child; scissors

Instruct children to cut the squares along the dotted lines. Ask them to look carefully at each word, paying attention to the ending. If necessary, review the word meanings. Direct children to put the word squares next to each other in order on their desks and say each word group. Remind children to use the picture clues. Ask children to point out details in the illustrations that helped them order the pictures.

**INFORMAL ASSESSMENT**

Direct the children back to the illustration on page 119. Ask volunteers to tell one fact that will help them draw the conclusion that bats help people.

## Vocabulary Strategy

**OPPOSITES**
Blackline Master 99

**Alternate Teaching Strategy**
Teacher's Edition p. T69

**INFORMAL ASSESSMENT**

### Objectives
• To reinforce compare and contrast
• To practice following directions

### Materials
One copy of Blackline Master 99 per child; pencils

Tell children that the pictures and words on the left side of the page (indicate with your hand) have opposite partners on the right side of the page (show with your hand). Ask them to look carefully at each word/picture pair and draw a line connecting it to its opposite partner.

Choose a word from the selection article, such as *in* on page 121. Write the word on the chalkboard. Next to it, write *real* and *out*. Have children tell which word is the opposite partner. (out)

## Vocabulary Strategy

**Review Antonyms**
Blackline Master 100

**Alternate Teaching Strategy**
Teacher's Edition p. T67

**INFORMAL ASSESSMENT**

### Objectives
• To develop familiarity with selection vocabulary
• To reinforce understanding of opposites
• To practice working cooperatively

### Materials
One copy of Blackline Master 100 per child; pencils

Tell children that the bat at the bottom of the maze needs to get to the cave at the top. Explain that each word will have an opposite partner next to it. Demonstrate by saying and connecting *small* and *large* for them. Instruct children to work in pairs to connect opposite pairs that will lead the bat home.

Direct children back to the article. Isolate the word *night* on page 119. Have a volunteer tell the opposite of *night*. (day)

# Bat Diagram

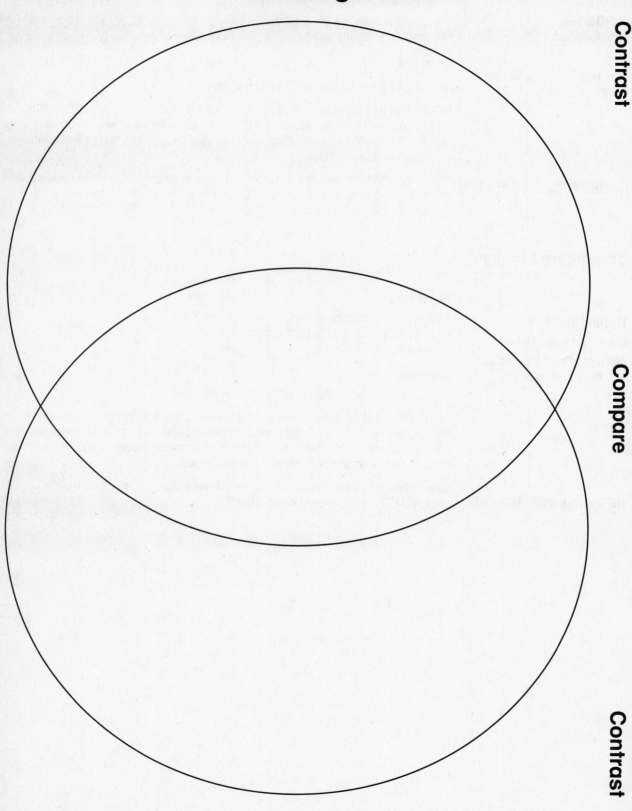

Contrast

Compare

Contrast

# Make Batty Words

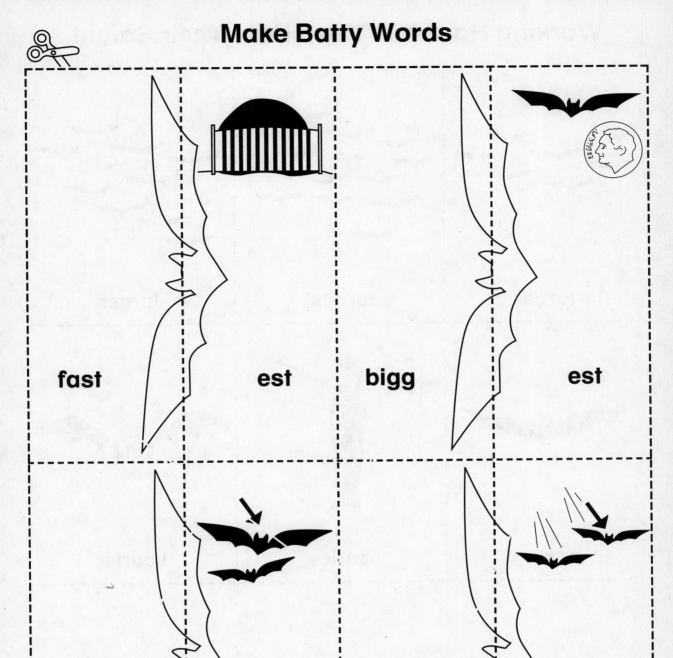

fast | est | bigg | est

saf | er | small | er

# Working Harder to Keep Bats Their Safest

**large**

**largest**

**larger**

**scary**

**scariest**

**scarier**

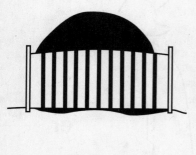

**safest**

**safer**

**safe**

# Connect the Opposites

big

safe

scary

many

few

tiny

# Coming Home After Being Away

home          away                phone

flower          cold                hot

up          dark          light

finger     safe     water     lamp

scary                    cup

square          quiet     large

hungry          forest          small

# THE BREMEN TOWN MUSICIANS pp. 130A–149R

The Brothers Grimm folktale  Retold by Margaret H. Lippert  Illustrated by Mary GrandPré

## BUILD BACKGROUND FOR LANGUAGE SUPPORT

## I. FOCUS ON READING
### Focus on Skills

**OBJECTIVE:** Listen for *r*-controlled variant vowels: /âr/, /ôr/, /îr/

**Alternate Teaching Strategy**
Teacher's Edition p. T64

**TPR**

### Develop Phonological Awareness

Tell children to copy your actions and listen for the /r/ as they repeat these words after you: *share* (mime dividing a cracker in two and offering it), *ear* (point to ear), and *four* (hold up four fingers). Tell children to listen closely and watch as you read the poem "Try a Little Music." Raise your hand after reading each word containing an *r*-controlled variant vowel. Ask children to repeat the word you just said. Continue reading the poem, encouraging them to repeat the words *scared, better, hear, pouring, your,* and *ear* after you. Then have children read the poem aloud with you. Instruct them to raise their hands whenever they say a word with the /r/ sound.

## II. READ THE LITERATURE

**VOCABULARY**
music
voice
whistle
scare
third
daughter

### Vocabulary

Print the vocabulary words on the board. Then read sentences from *The Bremen Town Musicians* containing vocabulary words. Invite children to guess the meaning of each vocabulary word, using clues from the sentences. For example, read a sentence from page 139 to prompt suggestions for scared: *The robbers were so scared by all that noise that they ran out of the house and into the woods.* Ask children to show you what a scared face looks like. For other vocabulary words, read the sentences from the story and do the following activities:

*music:* page 144, sing a short, familiar song with the children and say: *That was lovely music!*

*voice:* page 135, have children place their hands on their throats and sing the song again, say: *Your voice comes from here when you sing or speak.*

*whistle:* page 141, whistle the same song with the children. Explain that we also whistle to get someone's attention.

*third:* page 144, have three children line up. Ask other children to count with you— *one, two, three.* Then say: *You are first in line. You are second. You are third.*

*daughter:* page 135, show a picture of a family with at least one daughter. Have children name the members of the family, pointing out the daughter.

### Evaluate Prior Knowledge

**CONCEPT**

plays

Use puppets to demonstrate what a play is. Improvise dialogue from a familiar story with the puppets as characters. Help children identify the story. Explain that there are many ways to share a story: to read it, to tell it aloud, to draw it, and to act out or show what happened. Tell children that when a story is acted out, it is called a *play.* Invite children who have seen or been in plays to share their experiences with the class.

Discuss how a movie or television show is like a play. (It tells a story. Characters speak lines that were written for them.) Name a movie you like and then ad-lib a brief dialogue between two of its characters (taking both parts yourself). Encourage children to clap after your performance.

## Develop Oral Language

Organize children into small groups to act out a short scene from a movie, a story, or a nursery rhyme they like or that you name. Encourage the class to clap after each presentation, just as an audience would.

nonverbal prompt for active participation

• Preproduction: Name a familiar story. Tell children: *Show us* (point to self and class) *what happened when* (specific incident). *Show what* (name of character) *did then.* Have them mime one or more specific scenes from the story.

one- or two-word response prompt

• Early production: *Show us what happened when* (specific incident in story). *What did* (character) *say?* Encourage children to both mime the story and ad-lib simple one- or two-word responses.

prompt for short answers to higher-level thinking skills

• Speech emergence: *What story did you use to make up your play? Who else likes* (name of story or show)? *Have you seen a play? What play would you like to see?*

prompt for detailed answers to higher-level thinking skills

• Intermediate fluency: *Would you like to be in a play? Why or why not? What play would you enjoy acting in? Why? How do you think people in plays know what to say and do?*

# Guided Reading

### Preview and Predict

Read the title with children and take a picture walk through the illustrations. Stop at each illustration and ask children to name the animal. Look at the illustrations on page 141. Encourage children to guess who is whom. (Boss Robber, Muscles, and Curly) Then refer back to page 134 and point out the list of players. Explain that plays usually start out with a list of the characters. Read the list to children, and explain that these are the characters shown in the illustration.

Point out the unusual format of the words on the page, explaining that this is how a play is written. Identify a speaker name and say: *This tells you who is talking.* Then point to the body of text after the speaker's name and say: *This is what the character is saying.* Ask children to tell how a story and a play are similar and different.

Tell children that this play is about four farm animals that are too old to do their work. Encourage children to make predictions about the story. Ask questions to prompt predictions: *What do you think farmers do with animals that are too old to work? What could the animals do besides work on a farm? Where do you think the animals in the play are going?*

### Objectives

**GRAPHIC ORGANIZER**
Blackline Master 101

• To reinforce understanding of the concept of a play
• To reinforce understanding of main events in the play
• To support hands-on learning
• To encourage oral expression

### Materials

One copy of Blackline Master 101 per child; colored pens or crayons; scissors; four craft sticks for each child; paste or glue

Instruct children to color the pictures, cut them out around the dotted lines, and paste them to craft sticks to make puppets. On the chalkboard write simple sentences that children might use to retell the story; for example: *I am old. I can't work. I don't want to die. Come with me. We can make music. Let's go to Bremen Town.* Have children reading at grade level read the sentences aloud and then ask the rest to repeat the sentences. Explain that these are some things the animals in the play might say.

As you retell the story, refer to the illustrations and pause frequently, allowing children to hold up the appropriate story character and say the lines. Then ask small groups of children to use their puppets to retell *Bremen Town Musicians* to one another.

# III. BUILD SKILLS

## Phonics and Decoding

**REVIEW /âr/ are; /ôr/ or, ore; /îr/ ear**
Blackline Master 102

**Alternate Teaching Strategy**
Teacher's Edition p. T64

### Objectives
• To review words with /âr/ are; /ôr/ or, ore; /îr/ ear
• To build and read words with /âr/ are; /ôr/ or, ore; /îr/ ear
• To review initial and final consonants

### Materials
One copy of Blackline Master 102 per child; scissors; paste or glue

Discuss each picture with children, prompting them to use the target words *hear, scared, farmer, morning,* and *stored.* Give them these directions: *Cut out the boxes at the top of the page. These letters are missing from the words below the pictures. Find the missing letter or letters for each word and paste them in the right box. The words should tell about the pictures.*

If necessary, model trying out a letter or letter combination in a box to see if it works. Invite children to take turns choosing a word on the page and giving physical or verbal clues that will allow the others to guess what the word is.

Ask children to find the words in the play and tell what is happening.

**INFORMAL ASSESSMENT**
To assess recognition of words with *r*-controlled vowels, have children work in small groups. Tell them to turn to page 144, for example, and read any words they know aloud. Ask them to listen for words with the /r/ sound they've been learning about. Each group can list the words they find and read them aloud afterward.

## Phonics and Decoding

**REVIEW /âr/ are; /ôr/ or, ore; /îr/ ear**
Blackline Master 103

**Alternate Teaching Strategy**
Teacher's Edition p. T64

### Objectives
• To review /âr/ are; /ôr/ or, ore; /îr/ ear
• To discriminate and read words with /âr/ are; /ôr/ or, ore; /îr/ ear
• To review initial and final consonants

### Materials
One copy of Blackline Master 103 per child; scissors; colored pencils or crayons (optional)

Read the words on the page with children. Explain that each word has a picture that goes with it. Tell them to cut out the boxes on the dotted lines and find the boxes that have words in them. Instruct them to put the words in a row and then look at the picture boxes. Tell children to put the picture that goes with each word under the word.

Encourage pairs or small groups of children to play a game of Concentration. Instruct them to scramble and place the cards face down on the desk. Have children take turns picking up two cards at a time and looking for a word-and-picture match.

**INFORMAL ASSESSMENT**
Turn to page 139 and read the donkey's first sentence aloud. Ask whether children hear a word with an /r/ sound in that sentence. If they do, ask what the word is. Help a volunteer write the word on the board and underline the *r*. Continue in the same manner, reading aloud sentences from the play, until children have produced a list of 5–10 words.

# Comprehension

**INTRODUCE SUMMARIZE**
Blackline Master 104

**Alternate Teaching Strategy**
Teacher's Edition p. T66

### Objectives

Children will summarize a story by telling about its most important characters and events.

### Materials

One copy of Blackline Master 104 per child; pencils; colored pencils or crayons

Call children's attention to the heading over the first box. Read the heading. Instruct children to draw a picture in the box showing how some of the animals met. Ask them to think about why the animals met. When they have finished, read the heading of the right-hand box. Tell children to draw something that the animals did. Ask them to show something that was important in the story. Then read the third caption and instruct children to draw a picture that shows where the animals ended up.

Encourage children to use their pictures to retell the story to one another.

**INFORMAL ASSESSMENT**

Have children turn to the story illustration on pages 144–145. Tell them that the picture shows an important event in the story. Prompt children to summarize the scene that the picture illustrates in words or by acting out the scene. Encourage children to be brief when they summarize.

# Vocabulary Strategy

**INTRODUCE SUFFIXES**
Blackline Master 105

**Alternate Teaching Strategy**
Teacher's Edition p. T67

### Objectives

• To use derivational endings to help recognize and understand words
• To read and write words with suffixes *–ly* and *–ful*
• To learn how suffixes *–ly* and *–ful* change word meaning

### Materials

One copy of Blackline Master 105 per child; scissors; paste or glue

Write the words *quickly, suddenly, beautiful,* and *careful* on the chalkboard. Help children read the words aloud and talk about or act out the meaning of each word. Demonstrate for children how to cut out the word boxes, keeping the part of the page with the sentences. Instruct children to match the words with the correct sentence. Then have them paste the words in each sentence box. Pair less fluent readers with ones who are more advanced.

Have children write the words on cards and then cut off the suffix of each word so that it is on a separate card. Invite them to shuffle the cards and exchange cards with a partner to reassemble and pronounce.

**INFORMAL ASSESSMENT**

Have children turn to page 141 and find a word that ends in *-ly*. (quickly) Tell children: *Read the sentence to yourself. What does the sentence mean?* Repeat with this and other pages, having them look for words that end in *-ful* and *-ly*. Help them think of other words they know that end in *-ful* and in *-ly*.

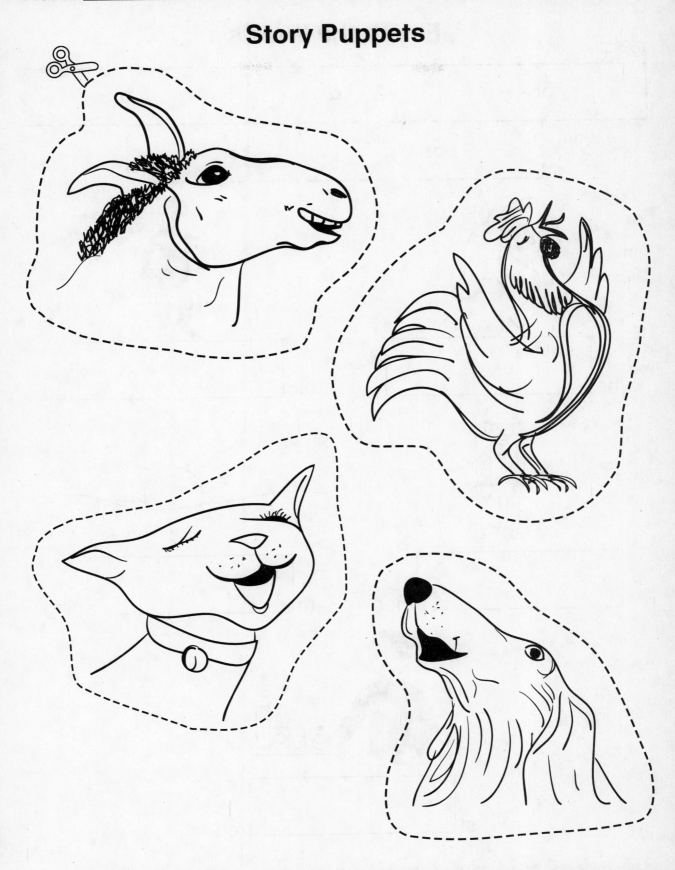

Name_____ Date_____

# Story Puppets

Name _____  Date _____

# Finish the Words

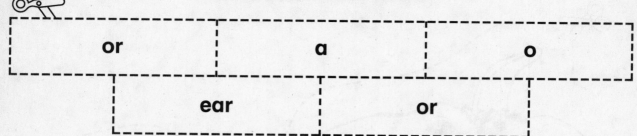

| or | a | o |

| ear | or |

he [_____]

sc [_____] red

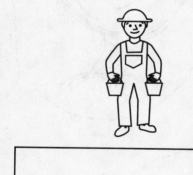

f [_____] mer

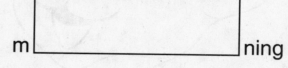

m [_____] ning

st [_____] red

---

**186** **Breman Town Musicians** • Language Support/Blackline Master 102          Grade 2

© McGraw-Hill School Division

# Word and Picture Match

| morning | hear | scared |
| stored | farmer | warm |
| story | | |

# The Important Parts

**How The Animals Met**          **What They Did**

**Where They Ended Up**

# Completing Sentences

| quickly | suddenly |
|---------|----------|
| beautiful | careful |

1. The animals all had [_____] voices.

2. The animals [_____] fell through the window.

3. The robbers had been scared away too

   [_____] .

4. The head robber told the big robber to be

   [_____] .

# OUR SOCCER LEAGUE pp. 150A–179R

Written and photographed by Chuck Solomon

## BUILD BACKGROUND FOR LANGUAGE SUPPORT

## I. FOCUS ON READING

### Focus on Skills

**OBJECTIVE:** Listen for /ü/ oo, ue, ew

**Alternate Teaching Strategy**
Teacher's Edition p. T68

**TPR**

### Develop Phonological Awareness

Provide each child with a blue crayon or marker and be sure there is an obvious new blue item in the classroom. Hold up the crayon and use the word *blue* to describe it. Tell children to look on pages 150 and 151 to find something *blue*. Explain that there is something *new* that is *blue* in the *room*. Say: *I will give you* clues *to find the* new blue *object in the room. The new blue object in the room is* (give a clue). Continue until the object is found.

After the object has been found, have the children repeat each word after you: *new, blue, room, clue.* Ask what sound is the same sound in each word.

Have children make the /ü/ sound. Then ask children to hold up their blue crayons each time they hear this sound as you read the rhyme "Game Time."

## II. READ THE LITERATURE

**VOCABULARY**
coaches
touch
score
field
stretches
throws

**CONCEPT**
team sports

### Vocabulary

Have children copy the words to make individual word cards. Dramatize each word and encourage children to hold up the appropriate card. For score, put two tally marks on the board and say: *The Falcons have two points. The Falcons got another point! I'm going to change their _____ now.* Record another tally mark. Have children take turns using or dramatizing the words after you have introduced each one.

Children can draw or paste appropriate pictures on the reverse sides of their word cards and take turns with a partner showing the pictures and guessing the words.

### Evaluate Prior Knowledge

Organize children into two or three teams and have them stand in a row, all facing in the same direction. Initiate a relay race in which an object is passed down a row. When the last person receives the object she or he runs to the head of the line. The game continues until the child at the head of the line is the one who was there when the game began. Talk about the game they just played. Explain that they were divided into two *teams*. People on the same team work together and help each other.

Display an illustrated book about sports and point out other team games. Encourage children to tell what they know about the sports that are pictured.

Name a team sport such as basketball. Mime dribbling and passing a ball. Say: *I play on a basketball team. We all help each other score points. Sometimes I am not close to the basket. Then I throw the ball to someone on my team.* Pretend to throw the ball to a child and indicate that they should "dribble" the ball and pass it to someone else. Ask: *What team sports do you like? Do you enjoy watching these sports or playing them?*

### Develop Oral Language

Invite children to pantomime playing a favorite sport. Have the class guess the pantomimed sport

nonverbal prompt for active participation

one- or two-word response prompt

prompt for short answers to higher-level thinking skills

prompt for detailed answers to higher-level thinking skills

- Preproduction: *Show us* (point to class and self) *a team game* (mime throwing a ball) *you like.* Child may pantomime the game or point it out in the book.

- Early production: *What team game do you like to play? How many players are on your team? Does your team have a name?*

- Speech emergence: *What's your favorite team game to play? What's your favorite team game to watch? Do you have a favorite team?*

- Intermediate fluency: *What team game do you enjoy most? What do you like best about it? What is a good name for a team? Why do you think so?*

## Guided Reading

### Preview and Predict

Tell children that this story tells about real children and a real soccer game. Display the title page and explain that the story pictures were taken at the game. Tell children: *These players are all on the same team. Their team's name is the Falcons. They are getting ready to play a game against their friends. Their friends' team is called the Sluggers.*

Lead children on a picture walk through the story, encouraging any who have played soccer to explain what might be happening in the photos. Ask questions such as: *How can you tell this player is not a Falcon? What are the Sluggers wearing?* Use the photos to help explain the concept of a team. Tell children that teammates work together (passing to one another) to score goals and try to stop the other team from scoring. Help students make predictions about the story. Ask: *Do you think the players are having fun? Do you think it will be a close game? Do you think the Falcons will win the game against the other team?*

Invite children who are familiar with the rules of soccer to explain and/or demonstrate the game to the rest of the group.

### Objectives

- To reinforce understanding of the main events of the story
- To support hands-on learning
- To reinforce working together cooperatively

**GRAPHIC ORGANIZER**
Blackline Master 106

**Alternate Teaching Strategy**
Teacher's Edition p. T69

### Materials

One copy of Blackline Master 106 per child; pencils

Draw the chart on the chalkboard. Open the story to page 154 and ask children to tell what is happening in these pictures. Encourage several children to respond and then agree on an answer for you or another child to write inside the first box; for example: *The teams start to play soccer.* Ask students who are able to write this sentence or a few words in the topmost box on their own pages.

Point out the score boxes on pages 158–159 and prompt children to tell what happens in the first half of the game. Continue in this manner, having them talk about the break, the second half of the game, and what the last page shows. Encourage children who are unable to write to draw a picture to go with one of the boxes.

To reinforce the skill of summarizing, have children use their charts or pictures to retell all or a part of the story to partners.

# III. BUILD SKILLS
## Phonics and Decoding

**REVIEW** /ü/ oo, ue, ew
Blackline Master 107

**Alternate Teaching Strategy**
Teacher's Edition p. T68

### Objectives
- To identify /ü/ oo, ue, ew
- To blend and read words with /ü/ oo, ue, ew
- To review initial and final consonants.

### Materials
One copy of Blackline Master 107 per child; pencils; colored pencils or crayons (optional)

Help children read the sentences one at a time, paying close attention to the words with the /ü/. Prompt children to tell or show you what the sentence means. Give them these directions: *Think about the sentence. The sentence tells about one of these two pictures. Which picture does it tell about? Draw a circle around that picture.*

If necessary, model choosing a picture to go with the first sentence. Children may color the pictures afterward if they wish.

**INFORMAL ASSESSMENT**

To assess recognition of /ü/words, have children work in pairs to find two words with this sound on page 178 or anywhere else in the story. Have each pair point out their two words and then use each word to say something about the story.

## Phonics and Decoding

**REVIEW** /ü/ oo, ue, ew;
/ôr/ or, ore
Blackline Master 108

### Objectives
- To review /ü/ oo, ue, ew; /ôr/ or, ore
- To blend and read words with /ü/ and /ôr/
- To review initial and final consonants

### Materials
One copy of Blackline Master 108 per child; pencils; glue or paste

Explain that the people in the boxes are saying something and that the words below the pictures tell what they are saying. Give the directions: *Each sentence is missing a word. The missing words are at the top of the page. Cut out the word boxes . Then use one of these words to finish a sentence. Paste the word in the box.* If necessary, read the words and sentences with children and model trying out words in the first sentence. Encourage children to read their completed sentences to a partner.

**INFORMAL ASSESSMENT**

Have children open their books. Using the words on the worksheet, prompt children to point to appropriate pictures and use the words in descriptions. For example: *Find a picture that shows a player booting the ball. Count the children in blue shirts in this picture. Count the children in white shirts. Are there more children in blue shirts?*

## Comprehension

**INTRODUCE SEQUENCE OF EVENTS**
Blackline Master 109

### Objectives
- To recognize sequence of events
- To reinforce understanding of logical order

**Alternate Teaching Strategy**
Teacher's Edition p. T69

### Materials

One copy of Blackline Master 109 per child; pencils; colored pencils or crayons; scissors, paste, newsprint

Explain that the pictures on the page show different parts of a soccer game. Go over the page with children. Encourage them to briefly discuss each picture, focusing on what the boy is doing and why they think he is doing it. Help them write a one- or two-word headline in each empty box, telling what is happening. Then have children color the pictures and cut apart the boxes. Instruct them to line up the pictures in an order that shows what happened first, second, third, and last. Invite them to paste the boxes to a sheet of newsprint.

**INFORMAL ASSESSMENT**

Read aloud one or two pages of the story to children. After you have finished, prompt them to recall the order in which the story events occurred. For example, read page 157 and then ask: *Who had the ball first—Eric or Toby? What did Toby do with the ball?*

## Vocabulary Strategy

**REVIEW CONTEXT CLUES**
Blackline Master 110

### Objectives

• To recognize and use context clues to find word meaning
• To practice using soccer vocabulary

**Alternate Teaching Strategy**
Teacher's Edition p. T71

### Materials

One copy of Blackline Master 110 per child; scissors; paste; colored pencils or crayons (optional)

Briefly discuss the pictures on the page and let children color them if they wish. Then help them read the words at the top of the page and talk about or demonstrate what each word means. Explain that each word goes with a picture. Have children cut out the words, keeping the part of the page with the pictures. Tell children to find a word that goes with each picture. Then paste it next to the picture. If necessary, model finding the word that goes with the first picture.

**INFORMAL ASSESSMENT**

Write the following list of verbs on the board: *wear, stretches, dribble, pass, kick, stop*. Read these words with the class. Then have them open their books to page 154. Read the sentences with these words, omitting the words. Prompt children to identify the missing word and explain or demonstrate its meaning.

# Summarize

[empty box]

↓

[empty box]

↓

[empty box]

↓

[empty box]

↓

[empty box]

# Circle the Picture

**1.** The player boots the ball.

**2.** You can play, too!

**3.** Boom! The player scored!

**4.** The blue team has the ball.

Name _____  Date _____

# What Did You Say?

| Score | boot | for | blue |

I ☐ the ball.

I am the coach ☐ the Eagles.

☐ team!

I play on the ☐ team.

# Soccer Sports Page

# Word and Picture Match

| stretches | throw | tie | score |
|-----------|-------|-----|-------|
| pass | dribble | field | kick |

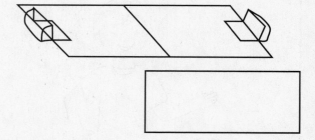

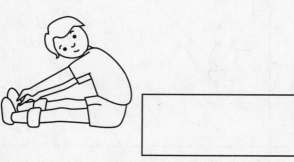

# THE WEDNESDAY SURPRISE pp. 180A–211R

## Written by Eve Bunting  Illustrated by Donald Carrick

## BUILD BACKGROUND FOR LANGUAGE SUPPORT

# I. FOCUS ON READING

## Focus on Skills

### Develop Phonological Awareness

**OBJECTIVE:** Listen for /ər/ er, /ən/ en; and /əl/ le

**Alternate Teaching Strategy**
Teacher's Edition p. T70

**TPR**

Display pictures of some women, a table, an apple, and a sheet of paper. On the board write the numeral 7. Ask children to tell you the name of each, and then write the word on the board. Finally, point to yourself and add *teacher* to the list. Tell children that the first part of each word is loud and the second part is quieter. Have children pronounce the words after you, loudly emphasizing the first syllable while stretching their arms high and then lowering their voices while dropping their arms as they say the second. Underline the letters *en, er,* and *le,* and tell children that these letters at the ends of long words are usually pronounced /ən/, /ər/, and /əl/. Read the poem "To Market! To Market!" and then have children repeat it after you, raising their hands each time they hear one of these sounds.

# II. READ THE LITERATURE

### Vocabulary

**VOCABULARY**
chance
favorite
nervous
office
heavy
wrapped

Print the vocabulary words on the chalkboard. Tell children that you will act out a story, using the vocabulary words. Ask them to see if they can figure out what the words mean.

*One day, Donna's father went to work in his office.* (if possible show a picture of a typical office, then wave and say, *"Good-bye! I'll see you soon!"*) *While he was away, Donna had the chance to make her father's favorite* (rub tummy and say yum!) *kind of cake. She made the cake and after it came out of the oven, she put it in a box. She picked up the box with the cake inside and said, "My, this is heavy!"* (pick up a box and show in an exaggerated way that it is heavy) *She wrapped her father's gift in pretty paper.* (pantomime wrapping the box in paper) *When she heard her father's car in the driveway, she got a little nervous.* (show a nervous face) *What if her father didn't like his heavy cake? As her dad opened the door, Donna shouted, "Surprise!" Her father opened his gift and they sat down together and ate the delicious cake.*

Write the sequence of events on the chalkboard, using the vocabulary words as guides. Invite groups of children to act out the story as you read it.

### Evaluate Prior Knowledge

**CONCEPT**
learning to read

In a big box, put examples of many kinds of reading material, such as text books, picture books, magazines, food boxes, holiday cards, menus, clothing labels, cassette boxes, and calendars. Say: *I'm going to pick a surprise from the box. Now you pick one.* Repeat the process so that everyone has two items. Have children hold up and compare their surprises. Ask children: *How are these surprises alike?* (All have words on them.) Have children identify any items they know the names of. Supply the unfamiliar names. Prompt them to acknowledge: *We can read (magazines).*

Discuss why people read these items in particular: *Why do we read newspapers?* Then discuss children's own reasons for wanting to read.

### Develop Oral Language

Invite children to trade surprises with a partner. Ask them to identify each new surprise and point to the words on it.

nonverbal prompt for active participation

- Preproduction: *Show us* (point to class and self) *your surprise.* Model holding up your item from the box. *Point to some words on it.* Point out some words on your own item. *Do you know any of these letters? Point to them.*

one- or two-word response prompt

- Early production: *Look at what I have. It's a* (name of item). *What do you have? What is it called? Point to something you would like to read. What is it? Can you read some things?*

prompt for short answers to higher-level thinking skills

- Speech emergence: *Tell us what you have. What can you do with it? How do people use it? Can you read any words on it?*

prompt for detailed answers to higher-level thinking skills

- Intermediate fluency: *What do you have? Can you read us something from the* (magazine). *Why is it important to know how to read the words on it? What would you like to read most of all? Why?*

## Guided Reading

### Preview and Predict

Tell children that the story is about a girl and her grandmother, who are preparing a surprise for the girl's father. Then use the story illustrations to establish characters and to reinforce the concept of learning to read. Look together at the picture on page 185. Ask: *What has the girl drawn on the window? Why do you think she did this?* Turn to page 186, and ask: *Who do you think these people are? What are they doing?* Look at the picture on page 189. Ask: *What are they doing? Why do you think they are reading? Do you think they enjoy reading?* Continue the picture walk until you get to page 196. Ask questions such as: *Tell me what you see on the page. Who do you think these people are? What are they doing? Do they look like they are having fun? Why do you think the girl wants to surprise her father? What do you think the surprise is? Do you think the girl's father will be surprised?* Have children independently or with the help of a partner write down their guesses about what the surprise will be.

**GRAPHIC ORGANIZER**
Blackline Master 111

### Objectives

- To reinforce understanding of the sequence of events
- To support hands-on learning
- To reinforce working together cooperatively

### Materials

One copy of Blackline Master 111 per child; pencils; colored pencils or crayons (optional)

Tell children to look at the sequence chart. Explain that the three boxes are for three important parts of the story. The first box is for something that happened in the beginning, the second for what happened in the middle, and the last box for what happened at the end. As a group, discuss the possibilities for box contents, and record keywords on the chalkboard. Be sure to introduce words such as *first, next, then, after,* and *finally.* Point out that these words help tell the order in which events happen. Children who are reading at grade level can write sentences to complete the chart. The rest can draw scenes in the boxes and, if they are able, write one- or two-line captions.

Have children use the illustrations or words on their charts as prompts to help them retell the story to one another. Remind them to be sure to tell about events in the right order and to use words such as *first, next,* and *finally.*

# III. BUILD SKILLS

## Phonics and Decoding

**REVIEW /ər/, /ən/, /əl/**
Blackline Master 112

**Alternate Teaching Strategy**
Teacher's Edition p. T70

**INFORMAL ASSESSMENT**

### Objectives
• To review /ər/, /ən/, /əl/
• To decode and read words with /ər/, /ən/, /əl/

### Materials
One copy of Blackline Master 112 per child; scissors; paste or glue

Help children read the words at the top of the page, and tell them that one of these words goes with each picture. Have children cut out the word boxes, keeping the bottom part of the page. Tell them to look at a picture and think about what they see. Then have them find the word that goes with the picture and paste the word box below the picture. If necessary, model finding the word that goes with the first picture.

To assess recognition of words with the /ə/ sound, have children work in pairs to look through the story text and find words that end with the /ən/, /ər/, or /əl/ sound. If necessary, have them look through other stories as well. Then ask them to share the words they found and read the context sentences.

## Phonics and Decoding

**REVIEW /ər/, /ən/, AND /əl/; /ü/; /ôr/; /îr/**
Blackline Master 113

**Alternate Teaching Strategy**
Teacher's Edition pp. T64, T68, T70

**INFORMAL ASSESSMENT**

### Objectives
• To review /ər/ er, /ən/ en, and /əl/ le
• To review /ü/ oo, ue, ew
• To review /ôr/ or, ore; /îr/ ear
• To build and read words with er, en, le, oo, ue, ew, or, ore, ear

### Materials
One copy of Blackline Master 113 per child; scissors; paste or glue

Use the same procedures you used for Blackline Master 112 to have children complete this page. Vary the activity by pairing fluent speakers with pre-emergent speakers and having them talk about the pictures in their native language before you discuss the pictures as a group. If appropriate, have children work in small groups to match the words to the pictures.

Look back at the story, and read selected sentences. Ask children to listen for words with r-controlled vowels and /ər/, /ən/, and /əl/. Give examples from the worksheet. Instruct children to raise their hands every time they hear one of these words.

## Comprehension

**REVIEW SUMMARIZE**
Blackline Master 114

**Alternate Teaching Strategy**
Teacher's Edition p. T66

### Objectives
• To summarize a story
• To review beginning, middle, and end

### Materials

One copy of Blackline Master 114 per child; pencils

Discuss the page with children. Explain that they are to summarize the story by dividing it into three parts—beginning, middle, and end. Point out that because the speech balloon is coming out of Anna's mouth, they should summarize the story as if Anna were telling it. As a group, discuss what might be written on the page. Some children may be able to independently write words or sentences in the balloons. If not, they can dictate sentences for partners to write.

**INFORMAL ASSESSMENT**

Encourage children to retell the story to one another from the point of view of another family member, such as the brother, the mother, or the grandmother.

## Vocabulary Strategy

**REVIEW SUFFIXES**
Blackline Master 115

**Alternate Teaching Strategy**
Teacher's Edition p. T67

### Objectives

• To define *suffix*
• To identify the suffixes *–ly* and *–ful* in a passage
• To write words with suffixes *–ly* and *-ful*

### Materials

One copy of Blackline Master 115 per child; pencils; colored pencils or crayons (optional)

For each item, read and discuss with children the sentences and pictures. Point out that the words that end in *-ly* give important details. Children may benefit most from completing the worksheet as a group. Read each sentence together. Encourage volunteers to tell or show what the sentence means. Then have children find the picture that goes with each sentence and circle the picture. Help them as necessary. Discuss how children made their choices.

**INFORMAL ASSESSMENT**

Ask children to find on page 200 of the story a word that ends in *-ful*. (wonderful) Discuss the meaning of the question. Write the question on the board, leaving out *wonderful*. Talk about how the meaning would change if you substituted *painful, fearful,* or *beautiful*.

© McGraw-Hill School Division

# Sequence of Events

Name _____ Date _____

# Cut Around, Paste Down

| candle | seven | brother |
|--------|-------|---------|
| water | dinner | giggle |

# Look for Clues

| | | |
|---|---|---|
| giggle | seven | morning |
| water | popcorn | hear |
| forgotten | brother | table |

# Anna and Grandma's Surprise

Name _____ Date _____

# Be Careful and Read Slowly!

**1.** Grandma vaguely remembered Dad's birthday.

_____

**2.** Grandma usually comes over on Wednesdays.

_____

**3.** Grandma reads each word carefully.

_____

**4.** Grandma spoke sternly to Sam.

_____

# FOSSILS TELL OF LONG AGO pp. 212A–235R

Written and Illustrated by Aliki

## BUILD BACKGROUND FOR LANGUAGE SUPPORT

## I. FOCUS ON READING

### Focus on Skills

### Develop Phonological Awareness

**OBJECTIVE:** Listen for /ou/ *ow, ou* and /oi/ *oy, oi*

**Alternate Teaching Strategy**
Teacher's Edition p. T72

**TPR**

Display pictures of a house, a mouth, a clown, and a cow. Prompt children to name what they see. Write these words on the board and have children repeat them. Help them discover that all four words have the sound */ou/.* Invite children to think of other words with this sound. Read the poem "Digging," asking children to raise both hands each time they hear this sound. Display pictures of or demonstrate words with the */oi/* sound, such as boy, toys, point of a pencil. Repeat the procedure above, having children listen for a word with the */oi/* sound.

## II. READ THE LITERATURE

### Vocabulary

**VOCABULARY**
buried
fresh
layers
millions
fossils
creatures

Use props or pantomime to demonstrate the meaning of the vocabulary words. Then ask children to say the words that are missing from each sentence.

*Animal bones that turn to stone are (<u>fossils</u>).*

*The bones of a fish were (<u>buried</u>) under the ground.*

*After it rained, the dinosaurs walked through (<u>fresh</u>) mud on the ground.*

*The mud piled up in (<u>layers</u>) to cover the fish bones.*

*Strange (<u>creatures</u>) called dinosaurs lived and walked on earth long ago.*

*Dinosaurs lived (<u>millions</u>) of years ago.*

### Evaluate Prior Knowledge

**CONCEPT**
natural history museums

Display children's artwork in a section of the classroom. Discuss the idea that this is a museum—a place where people can go to look at a certain kind of thing. Explain that this is an art museum.

Show some pictures of items that might be found in a natural history museum, such as fossils, bones, and extinct animals. Prompt children to identify some of these items. Help them understand that these are some of the things they might see in a natural history museum.

Describe a visit you have made to a natural history museum. Tell children about some of the exhibits you liked. Then ask them: *Have you ever been to a museum like this? What did you see there? What would you like to see in a museum like this?*

## Develop Oral Language

Encourage children to discuss real or imaginary visits to a natural history museum or other sites where nature was on display.

nonverbal prompt for active participation

- Preproduction: *Point to some things here* (point to example in room) *that you would see in a natural history museum.*

one- or two-word response prompt

- Early production: *Have you ever seen things like this in a museum? Did you see something you really liked in the museum? What was it?*

prompt for short answers to higher-level thinking skills

- Speech emergence: *What are some things you might see in a natural history museum? What would you like to learn more about? Why?*

prompt for detailed answers to higher-level thinking skills

- Intermediate fluency: *What was the most interesting thing you saw in a natural history museum? Why was it interesting to you? What did you learn about it?*

# Guided Reading

## Preview and Predict

Explain that this story tells about things that really happened. Display models of dinosaurs or a book of dinosaur pictures and encourage children's comments. Explain that the dinosaurs lived long ago and that we know what they were like only because they left bones and footprints behind. If necessary, use a shoe box with sand or salt to demonstrate what a footprint or handprint is.

Pair children needing language support with more advanced speakers. Then lead children on a picture walk through the story. Ask questions such as: *What kind of animal is this? Whose bones do you think these are? Where do you think the children are? Why are the fish's bones in the museum? What is happening in the first picture? What has happened in the second? How much time do you think has passed?*

## Objectives

**GRAPHIC ORGANIZER**
Blackline Master 116

- To reinforce understanding of a sequence of events
- To support hands-on learning
- To reinforce working together cooperatively

## Materials

One copy of Blackline Master 116 per child; pencils; additional drawing paper and colored pencils or crayons (optional)

Display the story map and explain that they will use their maps to tell how a fish ended up as a fossil in a museum. Discuss what should go in the top box of the chart. (For example: *The fish is alive.*) On the chalkboard, write the sentence or phrase children decide to use. Have children look at page 220 in their books, and talk about what sentence or words should go into each box. Reread or have volunteers reread page 220 aloud. The last box can show the fossil bones being found or being displayed in a museum. Some children may draw pictures instead. Encourage them to talk about their pictures.

Reinforce the skill of sequencing by pairing children who drew the process with children who wrote about it. Have each pair take turns using what they wrote and drew to tell the others in the class about the process of fossilization.

# III. BUILD SKILLS

## Phonics and Decoding

**SOUNDS** */ou/* **AND** */oi/*
Blackline Master 117

**Alternate Teaching Strategy**
Teacher's Edition p. T72

**Objectives**
- To recognize words with */ou/* and */oi/*
- To read words with */ou/* and */oi/*
- To practice following directions

**Materials**
One copy of Blackline Master 117 per child; pencils; colored pencils or crayons (optional)

Discuss the page with children. Explain that the sentences next to the pictures tell about the pictures. Read aloud the words at the top of the page. Tell children that each word completes one of the sentences. Point out that *soil* and *ground* are very similar in meaning. Explain that *soil* describes the dirt plants grow in. Mime picking up dirt and rubbing it in your fingers. Then explain that we use the word *ground* to talk about an area or place. If possible, point out the window to a playground or other areas of ground. Give children these directions: *Read the sentence. Then decide which word is <u>best</u> in each sentence. Write the word on the line.* If necessary, have children complete the activity aloud as a group and then color the pictures.

**INFORMAL ASSESSMENT**
To assess recognition of words with */ou/* and */oi/*, have children follow as you read aloud the second paragraph on page 220 and listen for a word with the */ou/* sound. Then have them point out and say the word. Repeat the procedure with the second paragraph on page 222, having them listen for a word with the */oi/* sound. Encourage them to use the words in original sentences.

## Phonics and Decoding

**SOUNDS** */ou/, /oi/, /ər/, /ən/, /əl/*
Blackline Master 118

**Alternate Teaching Strategy**
Teacher's Edition p. T70, T72

**Objectives**
- To recognize words with */ər/, /ən/,* and */əl/;* and with */ou/* and */oi/*
- To read words with */ər/, /ən/,* and */əl/;* and with */ou/* and */oi/*
- To practice following directions

**Materials**
One copy of Blackline Master 118 per child; scissors; paste or glue; colored pencils or crayons (optional)

Briefly discuss the pictures on the page. Then help children read the words at the top of the page and talk about or demonstrate what each one means. Explain that one of these words goes with each picture. Demonstrate how to cut out the words, keeping the bottom part of the page. Tell children: *Look at the picture. Think about what you see. Find a word that goes with the picture. Paste it next to the picture.* If necessary, model finding the word that goes with the first picture. Invite children to color the pictures if they wish.

**INFORMAL ASSESSMENT**
Have children make a word card for each word. As you display art from the story "Fossils Tell of Long Ago," prompt them to use one of these words to talk about the picture. Tell children to hold up the card as they do so.

# Comprehension

**SEQUENCE OF EVENTS**
Blackline Master 119

## Objectives
• To recognize the sequence of events
• To practice following directions

**Alternate Teaching Strategy**
Teacher's Edition p. T69

## Materials
One copy of Blackline Master 119 per child; scissors; paste or glue; colored pencils or crayons (optional)

Discuss each set of pictures with children, and talk about what happened first, next, and last. Have them number the pictures 1, 2, and 3 to show the appropriate sequence. Then tell children to cut out the picture boxes and paste them in 1-2-3 order in the boxes at the bottom of the page. Invite them to color the pictures if they wish.

**Informal Assessment**

Have children work with partners. Each partner should select one set of cards and tell what is happening in it, adding details she or he recalls from reading the selection.

# Vocabulary Strategy

**CONTEXT CLUES**
Blackline Master 120

## Objectives
• To put words in the context of pictures
• To practice using new vocabulary

**Alternate Teaching Strategy**
Teacher's Edition p. T71

## Materials
One copy of Blackline Master 120 per child; pencils

Discuss the pictures in the right-hand column with children, prompting them to use words from the left-hand column. Read the words aloud and explain: *Each word goes with one of the pictures. Draw a line from the picture to the word it goes with.* For children who are not able to begin the activity independently, model matching the word *coal* to the picture of coal, and then read the words aloud again. Encourage children to explain what each picture word has to do with the topic of fossils.

**INFORMAL ASSESSMENT**

Have children open their books and then use their hands to isolate the word *swallowed* on page 216. Say: *Let's read the sentences and look at the picture to figure out what this word means.* Discuss the meaning of the word. Then have pairs of children take turns finding words for one another to tell the meaning.

# Story Map

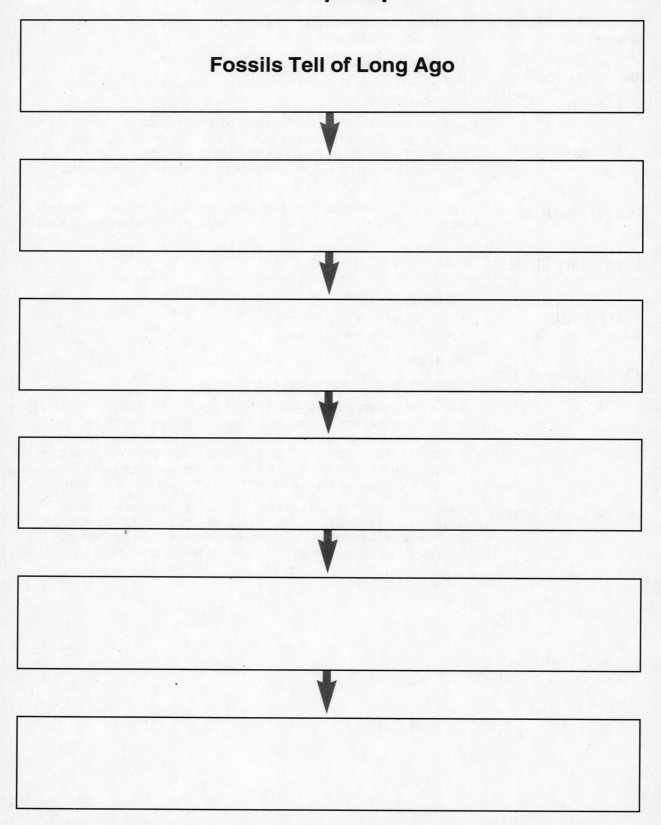

Fossils Tell of Long Ago

# Fossil Moments

| soil | mouth | ground | found |

_____

1. I _____
a fossil!

2. This dinosaur had a big

_____

_____.

3. Peat is a kind of swampy forest

_____

_____.

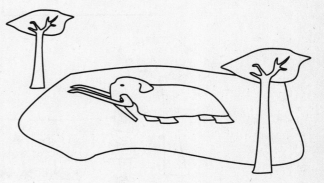

4. The mammoth was found in
the frozen

_____

_____.

# Match It

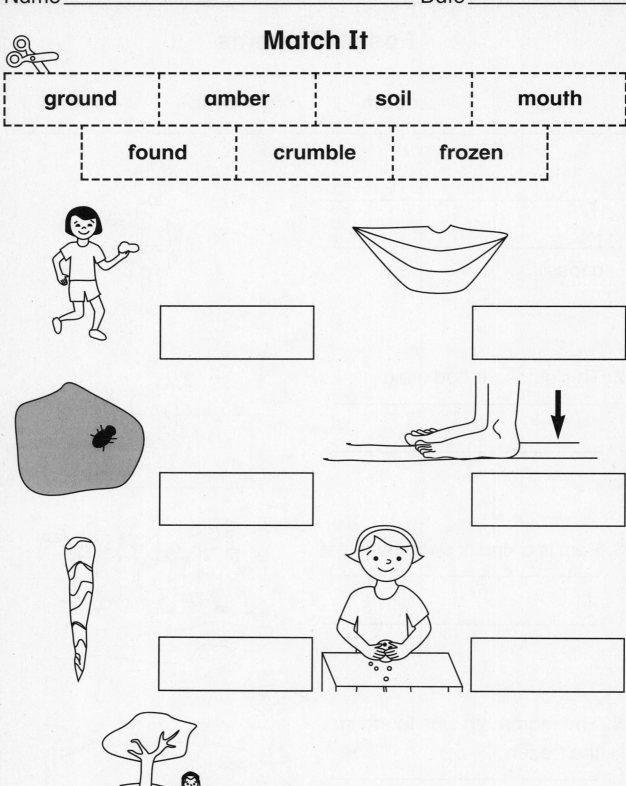

# 1, 2, 3 Fossils

# Matching Up

coal

layers

sap

mammoth

fossil

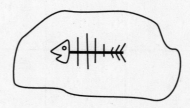

imprint

Time For Kids

## BUILD BACKGROUND FOR LANGUAGE SUPPORT

# I. FOCUS ON READING

## Focus on Skills

**OBJECTIVE:** Listen for *r*-controlled vowel /âr/; /oi/, and /ü/

**Alternate Teaching Strategy**
Teacher's Edition pp. T64, T68, T72

**TPR**

### Develop Phonological Awareness

Write the words *bark*, *point*, and *shoe* on the chalkboard. Say each word and demonstrate by barking like a dog, then pointing, and then touching your shoe. Emphasize the */ar/, /oi/* and */ü/* sound in each word. Have children repeat the words after you and mimic your actions. Say the following sentences and tell children to listen for a word that has one of these sounds. They should bark, point, or touch their shoes, to indicate which sound they hear. *My favorite color is blue. Joseph is a boy. I like to play in the park.*

Then read the poem, "When You're an Archeologist" and have children listen for words with those same sounds. Tell them to show you what sound they hear by performing the same actions as above.

# II. READ THE LITERATURE

### Vocabulary

**VOCABULARY**
hunt
magazine
piece
glue
tooth
change

Print the vocabulary words on the chalkboard. Demonstrate each word in the following way:

*Hunt:* Tell children that to hunt for something means that you look for it. Before class, hide a hat somewhere in the room. Say: *I can't find my hat. Will you help me hunt for it?* Ask children to respond: *We'll hunt for it.* Let children go on a hat hunt in the classroom until someone finds it.

*Magazine:* Bring in a variety of magazines that would interest children. Invite them to look the magazines over and then tell you which is their favorite one by saying: *My favorite magazine is _____.*

*Piece:* Have available an easy puzzle. Hold up a piece and say: *I think this piece goes here.* Give each child a piece and ask them to do the same.

*Glue:* Give each child a small strip of construction paper and take one for yourself. Glue the two ends of one strip to make a loop. Let each child do the same with his strip, linking one to the other to make a chain. Ask each child to say: *I will glue my loop to yours.*

*Tooth:* Point to your tooth and then say: *This is my tooth.* Ask each child to do the same.

*Changed:* Tell children to show you a happy face. Then say: *Let's change the way we look.* Demonstrate by looking sad, or scared, or angry. Say: *I changed my face from happy to _____.* Ask each child to respond in the same way.

## CONCEPT
fossils

### Evaluate Prior Knowledge

Display books and posters that show the bones and other fossilized remains of prehistoric animals. As you point out bones, discuss whose bones they are. Tell children about any similar fossil remains you have seen in museums. Point out a fossilized print and tell children that it is a fossil print made on a rock.

Discuss fossils by letting children point out pictures they are interested in or by acting out what they know about prehistoric life.

### Develop Oral Language

Simulate the formation of a fossil. Have children form their handprints modeling in clay. Allow the clay to dry and harden. Discuss how these handprints are like fossils.

nonverbal prompt for active participation

- Preproduction: *Show us* (point to class and self) *a dinosaur. Show us how a dinosaur leaves footprints* (display picture in book) *behind.*

one- or two-word response prompt

- Early production: *Whose bones do you think these are? Are the dinosaurs still alive?*

prompt for short answers to higher-level thinking skills

- Speech emergence: *How old can fossils be? Have you ever seen fossils in a museum? Where? What kinds of fossils did you see?*

prompt for detailed answers to higher-level thinking skills

- Intermediate fluency: *How do people find fossils? What would you do if you found a fossil? Why?*

## Guided Reading

### Preview and Predict

Tell children that this is a true story about a real person named Sam Girouard. Explain that Sam is a young scientist who is very interested in the plants and animals that were on Earth millions of years ago. Lead children on a picture walk through the article. Ask questions such as: *What do you think this is a picture of? What do you think Sam is doing in this picture? Why do you think he's doing this? These pictures show fossils. What plants or animals do you see in the fossils? Do you think these fossils belong to Sam? Why or why not?*

### Objectives

## GRAPHIC ORGANIZER
Blackline Master 121

- To describe a sequence of events
- To reinforce working together cooperatively

### Materials

One copy of Blackline Master 121 per child; pencils; paper; colored pencils or crayons (optional)

Reread the first paragraph on page 240 with children. Then explain that they are going to use the chart to tell what Sam did on the day he found the tooth. Remind children to tell the things that Sam did in the right order. If necessary, model how to decide the event for the first box. Begin with *Sam was digging for fossils.* End by asking, *What do you think Sam did with the dinosaur tooth?* Invite children to write or draw their answers in the last box. (Sam took the tooth to a museum; Sam kept the tooth in a box) Encourage the more proficient writers to write brief descriptions or sentences that tell about each occurrence. Children needing language support can draw what happened on separate sheets of paper.

# III. BUILD SKILLS

## Comprehension

### REVIEW SEQUENCE OF EVENTS
Blackline Master 122

**Alternate Teaching Strategy**
Teacher's Edition p. T69

**INFORMAL ASSESSMENT**

**Objectives**
• To review sequence of events
• To practice using new vocabulary

**Materials**
One copy of Blackline Master 122 per child; scissors; paste or glue

Help children read the words aloud and discuss the meaning of each. Then have children talk about what they see in the picture, prompting them to use the words from the boxes. Give these directions: *Each word goes with one of the pictures. Cut out the four word boxes. Find the picture the word goes with. Paste the word under the picture.* If necessary, model matching the word *dinosaur* to the picture of the dinosaur. Then have pairs of children use the completed pictures to retell the story in sequential order. If necessary, model the first step. Say: *First the dinosaur died.* Then ask: *What happened next?*

Direct children to the second paragraph on page 241 of the story. Ask them to tell you what happens first: *Does Sam find a fossil, or does he write about it?*. Ask what happens after he writes about it. (Scientists read the magazine.)

## Comprehension

### REVIEW SUMMARIZING
Blackline Master 123

**Alternate Teaching Strategy**
Teacher's Edition p. T66

**INFORMAL ASSESSMENT**

**Objectives**
• To review summarizing
• To practice following directions

**Materials**
One copy of Blackline Master 123 per child; scissors; paste or glue; colored pencils or crayons

Discuss with children what is happening in each set of pictures. Talk about what happened first, next, and last. Explain that when you summarize you tell the important parts in order. Have them number the pictures 1, 2, and 3 to show the appropriate sequence. Give children these directions: *Cut out the boxes with pictures. Paste them in the empty boxes in 1-2-3 order.* Children can then work with a partner to summarize what happened in each set of pictures.

Have children look at the first paragraph on page 239. Ask them to summarize by telling the most important things that happened to Sam when he was eight years old.

# Vocabulary Strategy

**REVIEW CONTEXT CLUES**
Blackline Master 124

**Alternate Teaching Strategy**
Teacher's Edition pp. T67, T71

## Objectives
• To use context clues to determine meanings
• To reinforce using words with the suffix *-ly*
• To work cooperatively

## Materials

One copy of Blackline Master 124 per child; pencils; colored pencils or crayons (optional)

Read aloud the words in the word bank with children. If necessary, help them determine the root of each word and demonstrate its meaning. Give these directions to children who are able to work independently: *Each sentence is missing one word. The word tells how something was done. Find the word above that fits best in the sentence. Write it on the line.* Remind children that words that end in *-ly* often tell how something is done. Read each sentence together. Ask questions such as: *How do you think scientists do their work?* Help children choose a word and write it on the line.

**INFORMAL ASSESSMENT**

Write words such as *carefully, cheerfully, skillfully, neatly,* and *proudly* on the chalkboard and read them with children. Use the words in context and have children guess their meanings. Have children use these words to talk about the story.

# Vocabulary Strategy

**SUFFIX *-ful***
Blackline Master 125

## Objectives
• To reinforce recognizing and reading words with the suffix *-ful*
• To practice word identification

## Materials
One copy of Blackline Master 125 per child; pencils

Help children read the words at the top of the page. Discuss the meanings of the words using body language and performing demonstrations when necessary. Give these directions: *Read the words at the top of the page. Find each word in the puzzle. Draw a circle around it. Then cross it off the list.* Model finding the word *beautiful* in the first row, and reading the letters across. Suggest that children look for the letters *f, u, l* in a row, and then check to see whether the letters that come before spell out a word.

**INFORMAL ASSESSMENT**

Write words such as *careful, useful, hopeful,* and *gleeful* on the chalkboard and read them with children. Discuss their meanings. Have children pretend to be Sam and use these words to tell a partner about a discovery.

Name _____ Date _____

# Sequence of Events

```
┌─────────────────────────────────────────────┐
│                                             │
│                                             │
│                                             │
└─────────────────────────────────────────────┘
                      ↓
┌─────────────────────────────────────────────┐
│                                             │
│                                             │
│                                             │
└─────────────────────────────────────────────┘
                      ↓
┌─────────────────────────────────────────────┐
│                                             │
│                                             │
│                                             │
└─────────────────────────────────────────────┘
                      ↓
┌─────────────────────────────────────────────┐
│                                             │
│                                             │
│                                             │
└─────────────────────────────────────────────┘
                      ↓
┌─────────────────────────────────────────────┐
│                                             │
│                                             │
│                                             │
└─────────────────────────────────────────────┘
                      ↓
┌─────────────────────────────────────────────┐
│                                             │
│                                             │
│                                             │
└─────────────────────────────────────────────┘
```

# Cut and Paste Fossils

| dinosaur | bone |
|----------|------|
| scientist | fossil |

# Show the Order

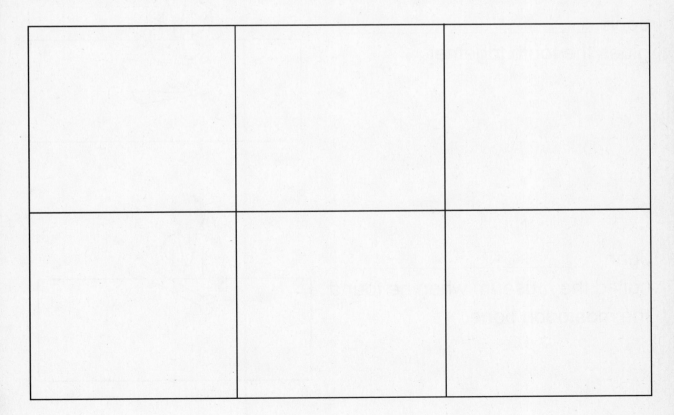

Name _____ Date _____

# Read These Closely

| quickly | seriously | gently |
|---------|-----------|--------|

Scientists take their work very

_____ .

John _____
glues the tooth together.

John _____
called the museum when he found
the mastodon bone.

# Circle the Words

| fearful | grateful | beautiful | plentiful |
|---------|----------|-----------|-----------|
| thoughtful | awful | joyful | |

```
x w i b e a u t i f u l a s c t i
s c o c r b d h p l e n t i f u l
a a c s e m a o c k n c y u l o d
n r a p i w l u q e f a z c b m r
r e s q z a v g r a t e f u l v e
i f c e b v a h f r w s r f l x f
f u q z c p c t s r a a w f u l t
p l d g r y q f e a r f u l w a s
s i y w e t a u a r t h n y a l n
p l i n o t b l p m j o y f u l q
t i t h o u g h t f u l n y l a j
```

# OFFICER BUCKLE AND GLORIA pp. 250A–281R

Written and illustrated by Peggy Rathmann

**BUILD BACKGROUND FOR LANGUAGE SUPPORT**

## I. FOCUS ON READING

### Focus on Skills

**OBJECTIVE:** Listen for digraphs *ch, ph, tch*

**Alternate Teaching Strategy**
Teacher's Edition p. T64

**TPR**

### Develop Phonological Awareness

Write these words on the chalkboard and have children discuss and demonstrate their meanings: *catch, scratch, itch,* and *kitchen.* Tell them that one sound is the same in all these words. Reread the list and have children identify the sound */ch/.* Then write *reach, march, touch* and *rich* on the chalkboard. Have children discuss their meanings and identify the sound */ch/* in the words.

Read the poem "Scratch My Itch" aloud and have children scratch their heads every time they hear the */ch/* sound. Have them touch their noses when they hear the */f/* sound. Repeat the procedure with the words: *alphabet, Philip,* and *phone.* Point out that the */f/* sound is spelled with the letters *ph* in these words.

Encourage children to think of other words in which they hear the */ch/,* or */f/* sounds and then act out these words for their classmates to guess.

## II. READ THE LITERATURE

### Vocabulary

**VOCABULARY**
accident
audience
cheered
slips
station
wipe

Show children the illustration on pages 274 and 275 of *Officer Buckle and Gloria.* Ask: *What is happening in this picture?* (people are falling) Explain that the picture shows a big accident. Invite children to share their experiences with accidents. Ask children what they think causes the accident in the story. If necessary, point to the carton of banana pudding in the picture and explain that someone *slips* on a puddle of banana pudding. Invite children to demonstrate the word *slips.* Ask: *What would you do to keep this accident from happening?* If necessary, prompt them by demonstrating wiping something off the floor and say: *Let's wipe this up.* Ask children to pretend they are sitting at a soccer game. Explain that they are the *audience.* Ask: *What do you do when you see someone score a goal?* Invite children to demonstrate by cheering. Explain that they *cheered.* Show children the illustrations on pages 254-255. Point to Officer Buckle's desk, his chair, the telephone, and bulletin board. Explain that the place where he works is a police *station.* Ask children to think of other stations. If there's a computer work station in the classroom, ask children to tell what kind of work is done there. Have them pantomime the kind of work that takes place at fire stations, gas stations, and bus stations.

### Evaluate Prior Knowledge

**CONCEPT**
animals at work

Display pictures of a wide variety of animals that can be domesticated, such as dogs, cats, horses, elephants, cows, and camels. Show the pictures one at a time and prompt the children to name the animals and tell something they know about each one. Explain that some of these animals help people work.

Tell children about an animal that helps people. For example, show a picture of a cow and say: *This is a cow. The milk we get comes from cows. Cream also comes from cows. Can you name other things we eat that come from cows?* Ask: *What other animals work for people? What do they do? Draw a picture that shows an animal at work.*

### Develop Oral Language

Discuss places where animals play important roles in people's lives, for example, camels in the desert or dogs/dogsleds in the Arctic. Also mention the various work dogs do for handicapped people, on the police force, at airports, and so on. Have children show the pictures they drew and talk about or demonstrate the work these animals do.

nonverbal prompt for active participation

one- or two-word response prompt

prompt for short answers to higher-level thinking skills

prompt for detailed answers to higher-level thinking skills

- Preproduction: *Show us your picture. You be the (horse). Show us what the horse does.*

- Early production: *What animal is that? Where is it? Have you ever seen it yourself?*

- Speech emergence: *What is that animal doing? How does it help people?*

- Intermediate fluency: *How does the animal learn to do that? What are some other things this animal could do? Are there other animals that could do the same job?*

## Guided Reading

### Preview and Predict

Explain that this story is about a policeman, Officer Buckle, who talks to school-children about safety. Tell them that Officer Buckle's speeches are so boring that no one listens, but all that changes when Officer Buckle gets a police dog named Gloria. Gloria goes with Officer Buckle and makes his speeches more enjoyable for the children. Take a picture walk through the story, using the illustrations to reinforce the concept of animals at work. Ask questions such as: *Does this picture show Officer Buckle learning a new safety rule? What do you think that safety rule is? Are the children enjoying his talk? Why do you think this? Do you think the people in this school need to learn safety tips? Why do you think the children are paying attention now? Do you think Officer Buckle knows what Gloria is doing? How do you think he will feel when he finds out? What does Gloria do for work? How does she help people?*

**GRAPHIC ORGANIZER**
Blackline Master 126

### Objectives
- To reinforce understanding of story main events and details
- To support hands-on learning
- To encourage creative thinking

### Materials

One copy of Blackline Master 126 per child; colored pencils or crayons; scissors; paste; craft sticks; additional paper

Have children color and cut out the puppet bodies and then paste them to craft sticks. Discuss whether Gloria looks like a good dog in the picture and whether Gloria always sits this quietly. Have children draw a picture of Gloria acting silly to paste it on the other side of the Gloria puppet. Organize children into small groups and let them take turns playing Officer Buckle, Gloria, and the school audience as they stage a scene from the story. Help them to come up with some safety tips for Officer Buckle to share with his audience.

Reinforce the skill of main events and story details. Have children use their puppets to show what Gloria is like without Officer Buckle, and what he is like without her.

# III. BUILD SKILLS

## Phonics and Decoding

**REVIEW DIGRAPHS *ph, tch, ch***
Blackline Master 127

**Alternate Teaching Strategy**
Teacher's Edition TE p. T64

### Objectives
• To identify digraphs *ph, tch, ch*
• To blend and read words with *ph, tch, ch*

### Materials
One copy of Blackline Master 127 per child; pencils; colored pencils or crayons (optional)

Help children read the words aloud and discuss or demonstrate the meaning of each. Then encourage them to use the words from the boxes above to talk about what they see in the pictures. Give the directions: *Each word goes with one of the pictures. Find the picture the word goes with. Write the word under the picture.* If necessary, model matching the word speech to the picture of the police officer giving a speech. Pair children who need help with more fluent partners to complete the activity. Invite children to color their pictures if they wish and then share their work.

**INFORMAL ASSESSMENT**

To assess recognition of words with *ch, tch,* and *ph,* read a sentence from the book that has a word with the */ch/* sound. Ask children what word has this sound. Repeat the procedure for *ph.* Then have teams hunt for words with *ch, tch,* and *ph* in other stories in their books. Call on teams to share the words they find.

## Phonics and Decoding

**WORDS WITH *ch, tch, AND ph***
Blackline Master 128

**Alternate Teaching Strategy**
Teacher's Edition TE p. T64

### Objectives
• To recognize digraphs *ph, tch, ch*
• To identify and read words with *ph, tch, ch*

### Materials
One copy of Blackline Master 128 per child; scissors; paste; crayons (optional)

Together, read the nine words in the boxes at the top of the page. Discuss the words by prompting children to demonstrate where possible and use them in speech. For example: *We cheered for our team.* Have children cut out these words and spread them across their work area. Then explain that the words below are clues that tell about each word in a box. Tell children to read the clue, find the word that it tells about, and place that word in the box under the clue. Once they have matched word and definition, children can check their work and then paste the words on the page. If necessary, have groups cooperatively complete the activity or let children work with partners.

**INFORMAL ASSESSMENT**

Have children use the words to write sentences or captions that describe the illustrations in "Officer Buckle and Gloria." If they work in teams, encourage them to use four or five of the words.

# Comprehension

**INTRODUCE FORM GENERALIZATIONS**
Blackline Master 129

**Objectives**

Children will form generalizations based on details given in a story.

**Materials**

One copy of Blackline Master 129 per child; pencils; colored pencils or crayons

**Alternate Teaching Strategy**
Teacher's Edition TE p. T66

Ask children how they think people come up with safety rules. (They see others having accidents. They figure out what made the accident happen. Then they say what to do to keep the accident from happening again.) Read the safety rule at the bottom of the first chart. Give these directions: *Draw a picture in each box. Show what happens when people don't keep their shoelaces tied. Show what happens when they do.* After they have drawn the first set of pictures, repeat the procedure with the second safety tip. Invite children to share their illustrations and thoughts with one another.

Encourage children to talk about other safety tips given in the story *Officer Buckle and Gloria* and draw safety posters, similar to the blackline master.

**INFORMAL ASSESSMENT**

Ask children questions about the story that will prompt them to make generalizations. Have them look at the illustrations on page 271 of the story. Ask: *What do Officer Buckle's actions on this page tell you about how he feels? How had Officer Buckle been feeling about his job? How does he feel about Gloria? What does it take to get a group of children interested in a boring subject?*

Mention other safety tips from the story and ask children what happens when people do/don't follow these tips.

# Vocabulary Strategy

**INTRODUCE MULTIPLE-MEANING WORDS**
Blackline Master 130

**Objectives**

Children will identify correct meanings for multiple-meaning words through the use of context clues.

**Materials**

One copy of Blackline Master 130 per child; pencils; colored pencils or crayons (optional)

**Alternate Teaching Strategy**
Teacher's Edition p. T67

Read the first sentence and explain that the pictures show two different meanings of the word *rings*. Give the directions: *Listen to the sentence again. What does the word* rings *mean in this sentence? Circle the picture that shows its meaning.* Repeat the procedure with the remaining sentences. Invite children to color the pictures if they wish.

Encourage children to look at the pictures and think about the second way each word can be used. Have them use the word to describe what they see in the second picture. Those who are able can write their sentences.

**INFORMAL ASSESSMENT**

Find the word *tip* or *tips* in the story. Help children understand the meaning here, and then ask them to think of another meaning for the word *tip/tips*. If they have trouble, point to the tip of a pencil. Prompt them to use the word in a new context if they are able. Repeat the activity with the word *stand*. Then have children look through the story for other words with more than one meaning.

# Story Puppets

# Name the Picture

| | | |
|---|---|---|
| **speech** | **phones** | **checked** |
| **telephoned** | **watched** | **cheered** |

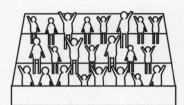

_____

_____

_____

_____

_____

_____

# Words and Definitions

| watched | cheered | checked |
|---------|---------|---------|
| telephoned | children | phones |
| chair | speech | speeches |

| something to sit on | opposite of booed | young people |
|:---:|:---:|:---:|
| | | |

| called | lecture | things that ring |
|:---:|:---:|:---:|
| | | |

| many lectures | made sure | stared at |
|:---:|:---:|:---:|
| | | |

Name _____  Date _____

# General Rules and Why

| Being Careless | Being Careful |
| --- | --- |
| | |

**Keep Your Shoelaces Tied**

| Being Careless | Being Careful |
| --- | --- |
| | |

**Always Wear a Crash Helmet**

Name _____  Date _____

# General Rules and Why

| Being Careless | Being Careful |
| --- | --- |
| | |

**Keep Your Shoelaces Tied**

| Being Careless | Being Careful |
| --- | --- |
| | |

**Always Wear a Crash Helmet**

© McGraw-Hill School Division

# One Word, Two Meanings

**1.** Officer Buckle's telephone rings.

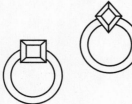  

**2.** Claire wrote Officer Buckle two letters.

 Q  Z

**3.** Wipe up your spill or you might fall.

 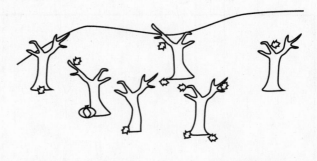

**4.** Keep your shoelaces tied.

# TOMÁS AND THE LIBRARY LADY pp. 282A–309R

Written by Pat Mora  Illustrated by Raul Colón

## BUILD BACKGROUND FOR LANGUAGE SUPPORT

## I. FOCUS ON READING

### Focus on Skills

**OBJECTIVE:** Listen for long *e* and long *i*

**Alternate Teaching Strategy**
Teacher's Edition p. T68

**TPR**

### Develop Phonological Awareness

Ask a child whose name contains the long *e* sound, as in *Kristina* or *Amy*, to tell the group her or his name. Call attention to the long *e* sound and ask whether anyone else has this sound in her or his name. Then prompt children to think of other words that contain the same sound. Do the same with the long *i* as in *Mike*. Read the poem "Magic Ticket," asking children to point to their teeth each time they hear long *e*. Reread it, having them point to their eyes when they hear long *i*. Help them recall words that rhyme with the long *e* and long *i* words in the poem.

## II. READ THE LITERATURE

**VOCABULARY**
borrow
desert
evenings
midnight
package
shoulder

**CONCEPT**
on the move

### Vocabulary

Print the vocabulary words on the chalkboard. Have available a book about the desert. Introduce the words with a child-assisted skit in which you say you want to *borrow* a book about the *desert* from the library. Tell them that you can go to the library after dinner because it is open *evenings*. Explain that you hope you won't stay up past *midnight* reading this interesting book. Put several books in a bag to make a *package* that's easier to carry and then carry it on your *shoulder*. Invite children to guess the meanings of the vocabulary words, based on clues in your skit. Have children re-enact similar scenes, using the new vocabulary words.

### Evaluate Prior Knowledge

Display a globe and a community map. Tell children that some people move several times in their lives. On the maps, point out some of the places that you have lived. Ask volunteers to name some places they have lived and help them locate and point out these places on the maps. Discuss whether they moved a short or long distance.

Tell how you felt about a move you once made. For example, say: *I was (ten) when my family moved to (Nevada). I was very sad to move. I had to leave my friends behind. I didn't know anyone in the new place. After a while, though, I made friends. Then I was happy there.* Invite children to talk about or display how they felt about moving from one place to another.

## Develop Oral Language

Encourage children to describe how they might feel if they had to move.

nonverbal prompt for active participation

- Preproduction: *Show us* (Point to class and self) *how you would feel (point to face) if you had to move away from (place name)*

one- or two-word response prompt

- Early production: *Would you have to leave your friends if you moved? What are your friends' names? Would it be hard to make new friends?*

prompt for short answers to higher-level thinking skills

- Speech emergence: *How would you feel if you had to move from here? Why would you feel like that? What do you like about living here?*

prompt for detailed answers to higher-level thinking skills

- Intermediate fluency: *What is the worst thing about moving? Is there anything good about moving? Tell what is good about it.*

# Guided Reading

### Preview and Predict

Tell children that Tomás' parents pick crops for a living and that once a year they must leave their home in Texas to go to Iowa to find work. Point out these places on a map. Tell children that Tomás' grandfather always moves with them. Tomás loves to listen to his grandfather's stories, but one day he discovers that he knows them all. Pair English-speaking children with less proficient speakers and take a picture walk through the story, encouraging children to think about what you just told them. As children answer your questions, have fluent speakers record the responses. Ask questions such as: *Why do you think Tomás is riding in the car? How late at night do you think it is? What are Tomás and the other boy doing? Who do you think this little boy is? Do you think the children are interested in what the old man is saying? What could the man be saying? Where is Tomás? Who do you think the lady is? Do you think anything special will happen at the library? What?*

**GRAPHIC ORGANIZER**
Blackline Master 131

### Objectives

- To reinforce understanding of how to make generalizations
- To support hands-on learning
- To reinforce working together cooperatively

### Materials

One copy of Blackline Master 131 per child; pencils; colored pencils or crayons (optional); child copy of *Tomás and the Library Lady*

Go over the chart with children. Explain that the box on the left is for important things that happened to Tomás. Page through the story as a group, discussing possibilities. Record possible key words on the chalkboard. Focus children's attention on how Tomás felt about moving and how he felt about reading. Children reading at grade level can complete the left side of the chart independently. Others can write a few words or draw pictures as the group discusses what happened to Tomás. Ask: *How can reading change someone's life?* Encourage children to answer this question in the right-hand box. Those who worked independently can share their answers.

Have children use the illustrations or notes on their charts to generalize about how reading might change their own lives.

# III. BUILD SKILLS

## Phonics and Decoding

**REVIEW LONG *e* AND LONG *i***
Blackline Master 132

**Alternate Teaching Strategy**
Teacher's Edition p. T68

### Objectives
• To review /e/, *ee, ea,* and /i/, *i, y, igh.*
• To decode and read words with long *e* and long *i* sounds.
• To review initial and final consonants.

### Materials
One copy of Blackline Master 132 per child; pencils; colored pencils or crayons (optional)

Discuss the pictures in the right-hand column with children, prompting them to use the words at the left. Have them read the words aloud. Direct them: *Each word goes with one of the pictures. Draw a line from the picture to the word it goes with.* You may need to model matching the word *peeked* to the picture of the boy peeking out the window or have children work with partners. Invite them to color their pictures if they wish and then share their work.

**INFORMAL ASSESSMENT**

To assess recognition of long *e* and long *i*, have children reread Papa Grande's story about the man in the forest on page 291. Tell children to name the words with long *e* and long *i*: (time, windy, riding, leaves, night, ride, teeth, finally, slowly, tree)

## Phonics and Decoding

**REVIEW LONG *e* AND LONG *i*; *ch, tch***
Blackline Master 123

**Alternate Teaching Strategy**
Teacher's Edition p. T64 and T68

### Objectives
• To review long *e: ee, ie, ea.*
• To review long *i: i, y, igh.*
• To review /*ch*/: *tch* and *ch.*
• To review initial and final consonants.

### Materials
One copy of Blackline Master 133 per child; scissors; paste

Together, read the nine words in the boxes at the top of the page. Ask questions that will encourage children to use these words, such as: *What do babies do when they're sad?* Have children cut out these words. Point out the words at the bottom of the page and say: *These words are clues. Read the clue and find the word that it tells about. Paste that word in the box below the clue.* If necessary, have the group cooperatively complete the activity or work with partners.

**INFORMAL ASSESSMENT**

Write the nine words on the chalkboard and assign one word to each child or pair of children. Have them look through the story until they find a picture they can describe by using the assigned word. If they are able to write, have them write captions to go with the pictures.

## Comprehension

**INTRODUCE MAIN IDEA**
Blackline Master 134

**Alternate Teaching Strategy**
Teacher's Edition p. T69

### Objectives
Children will connect main ideas with supporting details.

### Materials

One copy of Blackline Master 134 per child; pencils; colored pencils or crayons

Discuss the story with children, encouraging them to identify its main idea. Ask: *What do you think this story is mostly about?* Help them come up with a general statement for the main idea. Have them write this sentence at the top and on the right-hand page of the open book. Ask: *Name some things that happened that give extra information about the main idea.* Have them write these sentences under the main idea. Those unable to write can dictate sentences in English or in their native language. Ask children to draw a picture that goes with their sentences on the left-hand page of the open book.

**INFORMAL ASSESSMENT**

Remind children of the main idea of *Tomás and the Library Lady*. Then say several sentences, some of which are supporting details, and some which are not. If children hear a sentence that is a supporting detail, have them indicate by nodding their heads.

## Vocabulary Strategy

**REVIEW MULTIPLE-MEANING WORDS**
Blackline Master 135

**Alternate Teaching Strategy**
Teacher's Edition p. T67

### Objectives

Children will review multiple-meaning words.

### Materials

One copy of Blackline Master 135 per child; pencils; scissors; colored pencils or crayons (optional)

Have children read aloud the four words at the top of the page. Explain that each of these words has more than one meaning. Discuss possible meanings of these words. Then point out the pictures below. Give the directions: *There are two pictures for each word. Each picture shows a different meaning of the word. Find the word that belongs with the picture. Write it below the picture.* Have children cut out the pictures and place the two matching pictures together. Let children work with partners. Ask children to scramble the pictures and then have their partners match them again.

**INFORMAL ASSESSMENT**

Have children turn to page 287 in *Tomás and the Library Lady*. Ask them to find any word on the page with more than one meaning. (examples: *light, missed, bed, picked*) Then prompt them to generate sentences or to act out sentences that illustrate the different meanings of each word.

Name _____ Date _____

# Form Generalizations

| What Happens | Generalization |
| --- | --- |
|  |  |

# Matching Up

**peeked**

**read**

**pieces**

**climb**

**midnight**

# Find the Meaning

| cry | light | pieces |
| --- | --- | --- |
| photograph | teeth | library |
| leaves | teach | watched |

**what you chew with**

**these grow on trees**

**a building with books**

**sob**

**lamp**

**bits of something**

**give knowledge to**

**saw**

**take a picture**

# The Story of Tomás

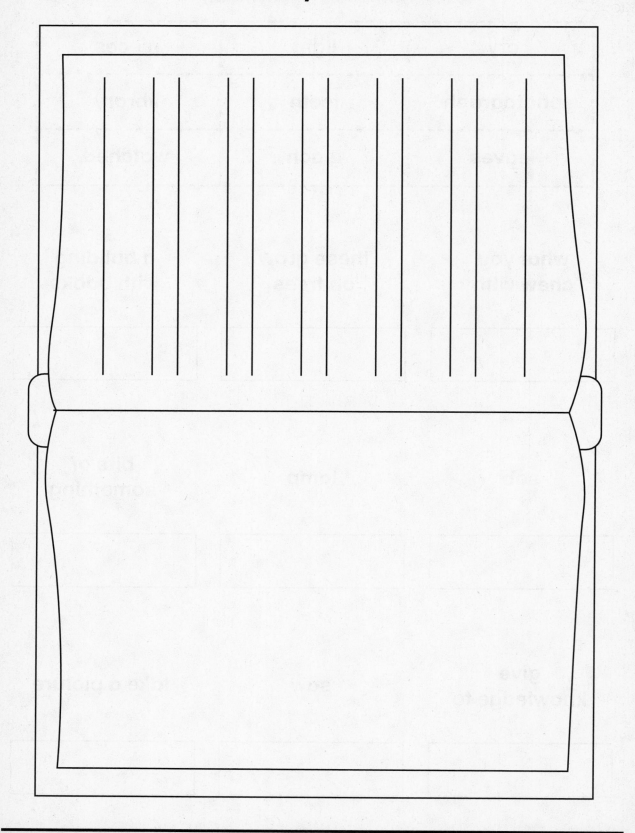

# Same Word, Different Meaning

| ball | windy | leaves | bear |
|------|-------|--------|------|

_____

_____

_____

_____

_____

_____

_____

_____

_____

_____

_____

_____

_____

_____

_____

_____

# PRINCESS POOH pp. 210A–339R

Written by Kathleen M. Muldoon  Illustrated by Linda Shute

## BUILD BACKGROUND FOR LANGUAGE SUPPORT

## I. FOCUS ON READING
### Focus on Skills

**OBJECTIVE:** Listen for long *a* and long *o*

**Alternate Teaching Strategy**
Teacher's Edition p. T70

**TPR**
Have children line up with a large open area in front of them. Read the poem "Little Sister." Have them take one step forward each time they hear the target sound—long *a* or long *o*.

### Develop Phonological Awareness

On the chalkboard write: *My name is Jane. I live in a cave. I play in the rain.* Ask what sound they hear in all the underlined words. (long *a*) Prompt children to think of other things that you can write about Jane, using a word with the long *a* sound. Repeat the procedure for long *o*. Write: *I am known as Joe. I live on a boat. I have a pet goat. I like to bowl.* Then organize children into two groups, one to listen for the long *a* sound and one to listen for the long *o* sound as you read the poem "Little Sister." Children make letter cards for their assigned sound and hold up the letter when they hear that sound. Have children switch cards, and then read the poem again.

## II. READ THE LITERATURE

**VOCABULARY**
princess
golden
world
cousins
restaurant
crowded

### Vocabulary

Print the vocabulary words on the chalkboard and use illustrations from books and magazines to introduce the new words. As you hold up each picture, ask children to guess what each word might mean. For example:

*Princess:* Hold up and discuss an illustration of a folk tale princess.

*Golden:* Hold up an ad for something golden, such as a car or a ring.

*World:* Hold up a photo of Earth or point to a globe.

*Cousins:* Define the relationships of a family shown in a photo.

*Restaurant, crowded:* Hold up a photo of a crowded restaurant.

Once you have introduced the vocabulary, have children write each word on a separate sheet of paper. As you show each picture, children stand, show, and say the appropriate word.

### Evaluate Prior Knowledge

**CONCEPT**
sibling relationships

Bring in a childhood picture of you and your siblings or of a set of cousins. Point out the members of the family and prompt children to identify them. (mother, father, daughter, son, sister, brother) Identify your sibling(s) and tell something about each one. Ask how many children have a brother or sister.

Explain that siblings are sometimes jealous of one another. Say: *Sometimes my (sibling) was allowed to do something I could not do. Sometimes my (sibling) got something new and I didn't get one. I felt bad and a little mad, too.* (Make a jealous face.) *I felt that my (sibling) was being treated better than I was.*

### Develop Oral Language

Ask children: *Do you have a sister or brother? How do you feel about her or him?* Have children draw pictures of their families. Help them label the members of the families with names and words that show their relationships. Encourage children to talk about their brothers and sisters.

<table>
<tr><td>nonverbal prompt for active participation</td><td>• Preproduction: Have children display their pictures. Prompt them to say their siblings' names and to point to various members of their families as you name them. Say: Show us (point to self and class) how you feel (point to face) about (name of sibling).</td></tr>
<tr><td>one- or two-word response prompt</td><td>• Early production: How many children are in your family? What are their names? Do you have fun with your (sister/brother)? What do you do? Do you get mad at (her/him) sometimes?</td></tr>
<tr><td>prompt for short answers to higher-level thinking skills</td><td>• Speech emergence: What are the names of your sisters and brothers? Who is your favorite? Why do you like (her/him)? Does anyone make you mad sometimes? Have you ever been jealous? Why? What did you do about it?</td></tr>
<tr><td>prompt for detailed answers to higher-level thinking skills</td><td>• Intermediate fluency: Tell us about the people in your family. How do you feel about your brothers and sisters? Do any of them get to do things that you do not get to do? How do you feel about that? What is the best thing about having brothers and sisters?</td></tr>
</table>

## Guided Reading

### Preview and Predict

Tell children that the story is about two sisters, Penny and Patty Jean. The big difference between the two sisters is that Penny has to use a wheelchair to get around. You might point out a picture of the wheelchair in the story. Tell children that Patty Jean is jealous of Penny because she thinks everyone treats Penny like she is a princess.

Take children on a picture walk through the story. As children answer your questions, write short responses on the board that they can copy on paper.

Use pages 316 and 317 to reinforce relationships and introduce characters. Ask: *Which girl do you think is Penny? Who do you think is her sister Patty Jean? Who do you think the other people in the picture are? How are they related to Penny and Patty Jean?* Continue walking through the illustrations. Ask questions such as: *How do you think Patty Jean feels in this picture? How can you tell? Why do you think she feels this way? How do you think Penny feels? Do you think she is always happy? Do you think Penny would like to walk? Why do you think Patty Jean is riding in the wheelchair? What do you think will happen to Patty Jean when she rides in the wheelchair?*

### Objectives

**GRAPHIC ORGANIZER**
Blackline Master 136

• To reinforce recognizing the main idea and supporting details
• To support hands-on learning

**Materials**

One copy of Blackline Master 136 per child; pencils; drawing paper

Explain that children are going to use this chart to tell about the most important idea of the first part of the story. Page through the story and discuss the most important idea of the story. Point out that Patty Jean thinks her sister Penny is treated better than she is. Have children write or draw this idea in the left-hand column of the chart. Ask: *How do you know Patty Jean feels this way?* Explain that children should write their answers to this question in the right-hand column of the chart. Tell children that these details help them to better understand the main idea of the story. Children can complete the chart with written text or pictures, according to their abilities.

Reinforce the skill of main idea and story details. Have children scan the story illustrations from the point where Patty Jean takes the wheelchair to the end of the story. Have them meet in groups to decide what the most important idea of the last part of the story is. Remind them to point out details that made them think so.

# III. BUILD SKILLS

## Phonics and Decoding

**REVIEW LONG *a* AND *o***
Blackline Master 137

**Alternate Teaching Strategy**
Teacher's Edition p. T70

**Objectives**
• To identify /a/ *ai, ay*; /o/ *oa, oe, ow*.
• To decode and read words with long *a* and long *o*

**Materials**

One copy of Blackline Master 137 per child; pencils; colored pencils or crayons (optional)

For children who can work independently, give these directions: *Each sentence is missing one word. Find the word from the box that is best in the sentence. Write it on the line.* Help the rest of the group read the words at the top of the page and discuss their meanings. Read each sentence together. Prompt children to choose a word and write it on the line. Children may color their pictures if they wish.

**INFORMAL ASSESSMENT**

To assess recognition of words with long *a* and long *o*, have pairs of children turn to the story and look for two words, one with long *a* and one with long *o*. Have them write each word on its own card. Partners then challenge another pair of children to read their word and use it to tell something about the story.

## Phonics and Decoding

**REVIEW WORDS WITH LONG *a, o, i,* AND *e; tch, ch***
Blackline Master 138

**Alternate Teaching Strategy**
Teacher's Edition p. T64, T68, T70

**Objectives**
• To review /a/ *ai*; /o/ *oa, oe, ow*; /e/ *ee, ie, ea*; /i/ *i, y, igh*; /ch/ *tch, ch*
• To blend and read words with long *a, o, e, i*; and *tch, ch*

**Materials**

One copy of Blackline Master 138 per child; scissors; paste or glue

Together, read the 12 words in the boxes at the top of the page. Prompt children to discuss and use these words by saying such things as: *Point to a window in this room.* Have children cut out the words in the boxes. Focus their attention on the pictures and say: *These pictures are clues. Look at a picture and find the word that it goes with. Paste that word in the box below the picture.* Model completing the first item. If children are unable to match the words to the pictures, work on the activity as a group

**INFORMAL ASSESSMENT**

Tell children: *Open your books to page 328. Find the word* window. Have children read aloud the sentence that contains *window.* Repeat this procedure with the other words on their worksheet: *read,* p. 322; *myself,* p. 326; *crutches,* p. 316; *rain,* p. 329; *field,* p. 328; *light,* pp. 326, 327; *day,* p. 314; *island,* p. 326; *sleep,* p. 333; *raincoat,* p. 319; and *chair,* p. 331.

# Comprehension

**Alternate Teaching Strategy**
Teacher's Edition p. T66

**REVIEW FORM GENERALIZATIONS**
Blackline Master 139

### Objectives
Children will form generalizations based on a reading passage.

### Materials
One copy of Blackline Master 139 per child

Remind children that every story has one or more important ideas in it. Explain that they can make generalizations about the important ideas by asking themselves what the story taught them or made them think about. Discuss one main idea: *You can't really understand what it is like to be another person until you stand in her or his shoes.* Some children may take this literally. Explain that it means you can't know how it feels to be someone else unless you do some of the things that person does. Then read the words in the lower boxes aloud and clarify their meanings if necessary. Tell children that Patty Jean had the experience of being like her sister. Have them cut out the pictures and paste them in the right boxes to show how Patty Jean felt before, during, and after her experience. Encourage children to imagine similar situations and discuss their thoughts about the situations.

**INFORMAL ASSESSMENT**

Tell children that another important thing they learned is that using a wheelchair isn't easy. Have them open their books to find examples that would lead readers to conclude this.

# Vocabulary Strategy

**INTRODUCE FIGURATIVE LANGUAGE**
Blackline Master 140

### Objectives
Children will identify and use similes.

### Materials
One copy of Blackline Master 140 per child; pencils

**Alternate Teaching Strategy**
Teacher's Edition p. T71

Pair children who have limited writing ability with skilled writers. Read aloud and discuss the four sentences at the top of the page with children. Point out the bottom four sentences and explain that these are about the same ideas, but in a different way. Tell children: *Read the sentence. Think about what it means. Find a sentence at the top of the page that means the same thing. Write it on the line.* You may want to point out that the sentences at the bottom exaggerate the real idea. Work on this activity as a group with children who are unable to complete it on their own or with partners.

**INFORMAL ASSESSMENT**

Call attention to the sentences *It is covered with cushions and feels like a cloud* (p. 323) and *I cover my eyes so I will not see myself go SPLAT* (p. 326). Talk about what these figurative sentences mean. Ask children to say the sentences in a different way to check understanding.

Name _____ Date _____

# Main Idea and Supporting Details

| Main Idea | Supporting Details |
|---|---|
|  |  |

# What's the Word?

| rainbow | anyway | maid | goes | raincoat |
|---------|--------|------|------|----------|

**1.** Sometimes Patty Jean feels like a

_____

_____ .

**2.** "She doesn't need her crutches

_____

_____ ,"

said Patty Jean.

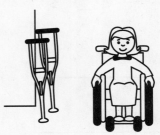

**3.** When it rains, Patty Jean wears an icky old

_____

_____ .

_____

**4.** Princess Pooh _____

to school across the street.

_____

**5.** When the sun came out, there was a

_____

_____ .

# Matching Up

| window | read | myself | crutches |
|--------|------|--------|----------|
| rain | field | light | day |
| island | sleep | raincoat | chair |

# In Someone Else's Shoes

| Before | During | After |
|--------|--------|-------|
|        |        |       |

# A Figure of Speech

| | |
|---|---|
| **I.** I, Patty Jean the helpful little sister, carry packages. | **3.** That's the way it's been for a long time. |
| **2.** Penelope Marie asks people for help. | **4.** Penelope Marie sits on her wheelchair. |

**I.** All day Princess Pooh sits on her throne.

_____

_____
_____
_____

**2.** Princess Pooh tells everybody in the whole world what to do.

_____

_____
_____
_____

**3.** I, Patty Jean the Servant, carry packages.

_____

_____
_____
_____

**4.** That's the way it's been for a million years.

_____

_____
_____
_____

# SWIMMY pp. 340A–361R

## Written and Illustrated by Leo Lionni

## BUILD BACKGROUND FOR LANGUAGE SUPPORT

## I. FOCUS ON READING

### Focus on Skills

**OBJECTIVE:** Listen for Soft *c: ce* and *g: ge*

**Alternate Teaching Strategy**
Teacher's Edition p. T72

**TPR**

### Develop Phonological Awareness

Write the words *change, cage, strange*, and *page* on the chalkboard. Read the words aloud with children. Help them recognize the soft *g* sound in the words. Then read the poem "Party Time," having children hold up a page of paper every time they hear the soft *g* sound. Repeat the procedure with the soft *c* sound, using the words *place, face, space*, and *race*. Have children cover their faces every time they hear the soft *c* sound in the poem.

## II. READ THE LITERATURE

**VOCABULARY**
swift
escaped
hidden
machine
swaying
fierce

### Vocabulary

Write the vocabulary words on the chalkboard. Introduce the word *machine* by pointing out simple machines in the classroom. (pencil sharpener, record player, etc.) Have children brainstorm other machines, such as cars, tractors, copiers, and so on. Introduce the other words through a narrated hand-puppet show. Say: *Once there was a very* fierce *lion. Everyone ran away when they saw him. One day he hid behind a bush to catch someone to eat. A monkey came along. He didn't see the lion* hidden *in the bush. The monkey was* swaying *back and forth on a tree vine when the lion jumped out. Luckily, he was a* swift *climber. The monkey quickly climbed the tree. He* escaped *from the lion.* Have pairs of volunteers act out the lion's and monkey's actions as you retell the story.

**CONCEPT**
sea creatures

### Evaluate Prior Knowledge

Show children an aquarium, a fish in a bowl, a video about sea life, and/or books about sea creatures. Then ask volunteers to discuss facts they know about creatures that live in the sea. Invite children who have been to the ocean or an aquarium to share their memories with the rest of the class. Write new vocabulary on the board.

### Develop Oral Language

Have children draw underwater scenes, showing some sea creatures they know about. Provide photographs of sea life to give them ideas. When they have finished their drawings, have them describe their work and talk about some of the photographs you have on display.

nonverbal prompt for active participation

• Preproduction: *Show us your sea creature.* (Model additional commands.) *Show how it moves. Show us how it gets something to eat.*

one- or two-word response prompt

• Early production: *Is this a little creature or a big creature? What color is it? Tell me one word about it.*

prompt for short answers to higher-level thinking skills

• Speech emergence: *What is this?* (Point to a picture of fish.) *Where do fish live? What do fish eat? Can you tell me more about fish? Have you ever seen a real fish? Where? Can you have a fish for a pet? Would you like to have a pet fish? Why or why not?*

prompt for detailed answers to higher-level thinking skills

• Intermediate fluency: *What is a fish afraid of? Suppose a big fish wants to eat a little fish. What can the little fish do? What do you think a fish does all day? What else do you know about fish? Would you enjoy being a fish? Why or why not?*

## Guided Reading

### Preview and Predict

Display the title page (pages 342–343) of *Swimmy*, and ask children: *What do you think the story is about? Who do you think Swimmy is?* Tell children that the story is about a little, black fish named Swimmy, who helps some other fish solve a problem. Explain that little fish like Swimmy often swim together in a group called a school. Find out whether children have ever seen minnows or other little fish in a pond or stream. Ask if there were several minnows swimming together in a school. Then take children on a picture walk through the story. Ask: *What is the big fish doing? Do you think he will catch the little fish?* Point to Swimmy. *Will he get caught? Here's Swimmy all alone. Why do you think he's by himself? What are little fish afraid of? Can you think of any way for Swimmy to solve this problem?* As you introduce the sea creatures, encourage children to comment on their appearance. Display photographs of the sea creatures to show how they really look.

### Objectives

• To form generalizations
• To support hands-on learning
• To reinforce working together cooperatively

**GRAPHIC ORGANIZER**
Blackline Master 141

### Materials

One copy of Blackline Master 141 per child; pencils

If necessary, lead children through the activity. Pair children needing additional language support with partners who can write. Tell children to think about the question: *Are fish the only animals that live in the sea?* In the right-hand column have children draw or write about some of the things that Swimmy saw under the sea. When children have finished, explain that these are story clues and that they can use these clues to come up with an important idea from the story. Have children share their work, and then ask: *What does all this tell us about life under the sea? (There are many kinds of animals in the sea. There are beautiful things to see in the sea.)* Write some key words on the board. Have children write their ideas in the left-hand column. After they share their ideas, list the generalizations on the chalkboard.

Reinforce the skill by having children take another look at the illustrations that show what Swimmy saw. Ask whether all of the animals are threats to Swimmy. Help children generalize that not all the creatures in the sea want to eat Swimmy.

# III. BUILD SKILLS

## Phonics and Decoding

**SOFT *c* AND *g***
Blackline Master 142

**Alternate Teaching Strategy**
Teacher's Edition p. T72

**INFORMAL ASSESSMENT**

### Objectives
- To recognize words with soft *c* and *g*
- To read words with soft *c* and *g*
- To practice following directions

### Materials
One copy of Blackline Master 142 per child; pencils; colored pencils or crayons (optional)

Go over the page with children, pointing out that there are two pictures under each sentence. Give these directions: *Read the sentence. Find the picture that goes with the sentence. Draw a circle around the picture.* Pair children who are unable to complete the page independently with fluent partners. Then read the sentences aloud together, pointing out the words with the soft *c* and *g* sounds. Call attention to how these sounds are spelled in these words. Encourage volunteers to use these words to talk about familiar topics.

To assess recognition of soft *c* and *g*, have children look in the book for words with these sounds. When they find the words, encourage them to use the words to talk about the story.

## Phonics and Decoding

**REVIEW SOFT *c* AND *g*;
LONG VOWEL SOUNDS**
Blackline Master 143

**Alternate Teaching Strategy**
Teacher's Edition p. T68, T70, T72

**INFORMAL ASSESSMENT**

### Objectives
- To recognize words with long vowel sounds, soft *c*, and soft *g*
- To read words with long vowel sounds, soft *c*, and soft *g*

### Materials
One copy of Blackline Master 143 per child; colored pencils or crayons; scissors; paste or glue and paper (optional)

Go over the page with children, and discuss what they see in the pictures. Invite them to color the pictures if they wish. Give the directions: *Cut apart the squares. Read the words. Match each word to the picture that it goes with.* Organize children into small groups to play "Concentration" with the cards. Have children mix up the cards and place them face down. Have players take turns picking up two cards and looking for a word/picture match.

Write on the chalkboard the words from the blackline master. Have children select two words that can be used to describe a scene from *Swimmy*. Then direct them to draw the scene and write the two words on the drawing. Have them display and describe their pictures.

# Comprehension

**MAIN IDEA**
Blackline Master 144

**Alternate Teaching Strategy**
Teacher's Edition p. T69

### Objectives
• To identify the main idea
• To practice following directions

### Materials
One copy of Blackline Master 144 per child; one red colored pencil or crayon per child; scissors; pastels; drawing paper

Have children color all of the fish except Swimmy red, as indicated in the story. Then tell children to cut out all the fish. Ask what they think is the most important idea in the story. Discuss their responses. (Example: *Together you can do things you can't do alone.*) Have children arrange their fish on a separate sheet of paper in the shape of a fish. Have them use the black fish for an eye. When the fish are correctly arranged, children can paste them down. Alternatively, invite children to put all their red fish together and make one big fish on a sheet of butcher paper. Discuss different activities children can do together that they cannot do alone. (play baseball, board games, etc.)

**INFORMAL ASSESSMENT**

Have children discuss *Swimmy* and tell what they think Swimmy's character is like. Ask, *Is he always scared or is he brave?* Ask what they think is the main idea that the writer wants them to know.

# Vocabulary Strategy

**FIGURATIVE LANGUAGE**
Blackline Master 145

**Alternate Teaching Strategy**
Teacher's Edition p. T71

### Objectives
• To understand figurative language
• To work cooperatively

### Materials
One copy of Blackline Master 145 per child; pencils; colored pencils or crayons (optional)

If possible, obtain some hard, glossy candy to make the description of rocks easier to visualize. Tell children that they are going to read some words that describe the pictures on the page. Explain that the words compare what they see in the pictures to something else. Give the directions: *Read the words. Look at the picture. What do the words you just read make you see? Read the words in the box. Find the words that mean the same thing. Write the words under the picture.* If necessary, guide children through the activity, using prompts such as: *Seaweed doesn't grow in forests. How could seaweed be like a forest of trees?* After children have completed the activity, invite them to color the pictures.

**INFORMAL ASSESSMENT**

Have children turn to page 346 and focus on the words *a medusa of rainbow jelly*. Discuss how a sea creature can be like jelly and what rainbow jelly would look like. Have children illustrate the phrase *an army of fierce sharks*.

# Form Generalizations

| Clues From The Story | Generalizations Formed |
|---|---|
| | |

Name _____ Date _____

# Circle the Picture

**1.** A fierce tuna fish came darting through the waves.

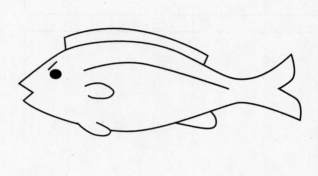

**2.** Swimmy saw <u>strange</u> fish, pulled by an invisible thread.

**3.** The fish swam <u>together</u>, each in his own <u>place</u>.

# Word and Picture Match

| place | strange | tail | day |
| --- | --- | --- | --- |
| rainbow | eel | eat | giant |

# Friends That Swim Together Stay Together

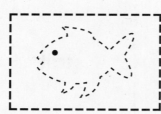
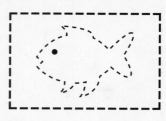

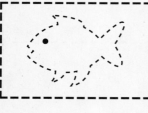
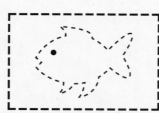
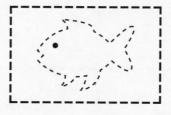

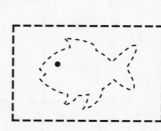

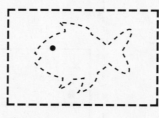

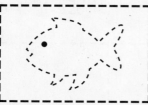
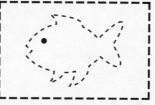

_____

_____

_____

_____

 Grade 2

Name _____ Date _____

# Figuring Out What It Means

| a very long eel | bright, shiny rocks | a lot of seaweed |
|---|---|---|

a forest of seaweed

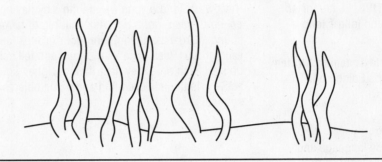

_____

_____

an eel whose tail was almost too far away to remember

_____

_____

sugar-candy rocks

_____

_____

# THE WORLD'S PLANTS ARE IN DANGER pp. 362A–371R

Time For Kids

## BUILD BACKGROUND FOR LANGUAGE SUPPORT

## I. FOCUS ON READING
### Focus on Skills

**OBJECTIVE:** Listen for *ch*, long *e* and long *i*, long *a*

**Alternate Teaching Strategy**
Teacher's Edition pp. T64, T68, T70

**TPR**
Use body language and physical response to demonstrate recognition of sounds.

### Develop Phonological Awareness

Review *ch*, long *e*, long *i*, and long *a* by having children repeat words such as *change, green, right, day*. Ask children to name other words they know with these sounds. Organize children into four groups, and assign one of the target sounds to each group. Read "The Plan" aloud and tell children in each group to show a thumbs-up sign each time they hear their assigned sound. You may want to do a similar activity, letting children find and name objects in the classroom which contain the sounds.

## II. READ THE LITERATURE

### Vocabulary

**VOCABULARY**
problem
disappear
cleared
warns
save
forever

Write the vocabulary words on the chalkboard. Together, repeat the vocabulary words and discuss their meanings. Then assign each child one vocabulary word and have them write that word on a sheet of paper. Give clues or meanings for the vocabulary, and tell children to hold up the sheet of paper and say the word when the clue refers to their word.

*Problem:* The world's plants are in danger and we need to save them. We have a _____ that we need to solve.

*Disappear:* People won't see the plants anymore. The plants will _____.

*Cleared:* Plants die when rainforests are _____. This happens when the plants are cut down to make room for buildings.

*Warns:* This article _____ us not to cut down or pick plants that are in danger.

*Save:* Some people are trying to _____ the plants by keeping them safe from danger.

*Forever:* If we don't save the plants, they could disappear _____ and never grow back.

### Evaluate Prior Knowledge

**CONCEPT**
some plants are endangered

Bring in a picture of a heavily wooded area and a picture of a developed area with a shopping mall, parking lot, etc. Ask: *What difference do you see in these two pictures?* Discuss what happens when trees are cut down and removed from an area. Ask: *Will they grow back?* Point to the picture of the wooded area and ask: *Imagine that this was the only place in the world where a certain plant lived. What happened to this plant when the shopping mall was built?*

### Develop Oral Language

Encourage children to talk about the concepts of plants and dying out. Display pictures of different flowers and plants. Mention reasons for plants disappearing, such as building, pollution, or people picking or collecting them. Talk about children's feelings about this topic.

nonverbal prompt for active participation

- Preproduction: *Show us* (point to class and self) *) which plants you think are pretty. Show me the plant you like best. Show how you would feel* (point to face) *if this plant disappeared.*

one- or two-word response prompt

- Early production: *Do you like plants? Which plant do you like best? How would you feel if this plant disappeared forever?*

prompt for short answers to higher-level thinking skills

- Speech emergence: *Which of these plants have you seen before? Can you name any of the plants in the pictures? What are some things that could harm plants?*

prompt for detailed answers to higher-level thinking skills

- Intermediate fluency: *What is the most interesting plant you know about? Why is it interesting? What would you do if you found out this plant was in danger of dying out?*

## Guided Reading

### Preview and Predict

Explain that the article children are about to read is about plants all over the world. Have children view the pictures and talk about the plants in them. Ask questions such as: *Have you ever seen plants like these? Do you like these plants? Why do you like them? Which plant has the prettiest color? Where are cacti found?*

Remind them that they learned that some animals, like the dinosaur, have died out; they have disappeared from Earth forever. Tell children: *Some plants are like dinosaurs. They can no longer be found on Earth. What do you think made them disappear? Other plants are dying out. There are only a few left today. They are in danger of disappearing, too. Why do you think they are dying out?*

### Objectives

- To identify the main idea and supporting details
- To practice working cooperatively

**GRAPHIC ORGANIZER**
Blackline Master 146

### Materials

One copy of Blackline Master 146 per child; pencils

Copy the chart on the chalkboard. Point out the left-hand column and explain that it is for the most important idea in the article. Ask children what they think is the most important idea of the article. Record their comments on the chalkboard. Then ask what the writer says to make readers believe that this is true. Prompt children to respond with details that support the claim that the world's plants are in danger. Ask: *How many plants are in danger of disappearing? Why are the plants dying?*

**INFORMAL ASSESSMENT**

Have children reread the last paragraph of the article. Discuss what its main idea is and have children identify the details that support this idea.

# III. BUILD SKILLS

## Comprehension

**REVIEW MAIN IDEA**
Blackline Master 147

**Alternate Teaching Strategy**
Teacher's Edition p. T69

**INFORMAL ASSESSMENT**

### Objectives
Children will identify main idea and supporting details.

### Materials
One copy of Blackline Master 147 per child; pencils

Remind children that the main idea is the most important information that the author writes in the article and that supporting details help to develop the main idea by giving other information. Have children look at the pictures and discuss what is being shown in each one. Then have them draw lines from the pictures that show supporting details to the picture that best shows the main idea of the *The World's Plants Are in Danger*.

Show children a number of photographs from a magazine or newspaper with the captions folded under. Ask them to tell you what the main idea of each photograph is.

## Comprehension

**REVIEW FORM GENERALIZATIONS**
Blackline Master 148

**Alternate Teaching Strategy**
Teacher's Edition p. T66

**INFORMAL ASSESSMENT**

### Objectives
Children will recognize and form generalizations.

### Materials
One copy of Blackline Master 148 per child; pencils; colored pencils or crayons

Pair less fluent children with more advanced readers as writing partners for this activity. Ask children to look at the pictures and write a sentence that is a generalization about each picture. Remind children that generalizations often begin with words such as *most, usually, some,* and *many*.

Have children discuss what they learned from this article. Ask them to think of a generalization that tells why plants should be protected.

# Vocabulary Strategy

### REVIEW FIGURATIVE LANGUAGE
Blackline Master 149

**Objectives**
• To review figurative language.
• To review simile and metaphor

**Materials**

One copy of Blackline Master 149 per child; pencils; colored pencils or crayons (optional)

Remind children that words will sometimes tell what something is like rather than exactly what the thing is. Give the directions: *Read the words. Think about what the words make you see. Draw a picture to go with the words.* You may wish to walk children through the activity by using prompts. For example, ask in what ways a field of flowers and the sea might be alike. Encourage children to share and talk about their drawings.

### INFORMAL ASSESSMENT

Ask children to look at the photograph of the raffelesia in the article. Ask them if it reminds them of anything else. Help them think of some figurative expressions they could use to describe this huge flower.

# Vocabulary Strategy

### REVIEW MULTIPLE-MEANING WORDS

**Objectives**

Children will review multiple-meaning words.

**Materials**

One copy of Blackline Master 150 per child; pencils

Go over the page with children. Tell them that they are to help the girl find a path that leads to the pretty flower. To get to the flower, she must only go through words that have more than one meaning. Model the activity: *I know that the path goes through* plant *because I know more than one meaning for* plant. *Now should I turn toward* egg *or* rose*?* Which word has more than one meaning? After children have completed the maze, help them review the meanings of the different words they passed. Ask whether they can see two meanings in the title of the page.

### INFORMAL ASSESSMENT

Have children look back through the article for words that have more than one meaning. (examples: *crowd, spot, pay, may*) Encourage them to use the words in sentences that make their meanings clear.

# Main Idea

| Main Idea | Details |
|-----------|---------|
|           |         |

Name _____ Date _____

# Picture This

| a sea of sunflowers | an army of bulldozers |
|---|---|
| a city of cacti | the jewel of the garden |

# In Your Own Words

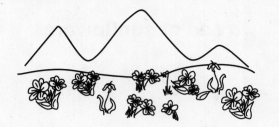

_____

_____

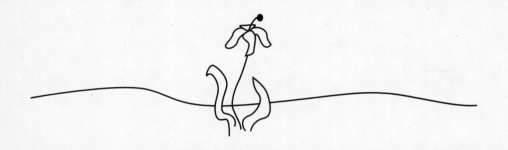

_____

_____

_____

_____

_____

_____

Name _____ Date _____

# Same Word, Different Meaning

| plant | rose | types | safe |
|-------|------|-------|------|

✂

_____   _____

_____   _____

_____   _____

_____   _____

_____   _____

_____   _____

_____   _____

_____   _____

# Go the Right Way!

Please
Do Not
Pick Flowers

nose

part

dog

leaves

three

rug

rose

plant

night

egg